Certifiably Insane

How the United States got itself into an endless shuffle through the bowels of Bedlam

By

Tom Reidy

Dedication

Dedicated to Leonard Goodrich who shares my intense dislike for the insane asylum that the United States has become and who suggested this title.

Preface

We are committing cultural suicide!

In this book we will analyze the reasons why American culture is in steep decline. Cultural decline is not only an American phenomenon; it is a worldwide event but we are going to focus primarily on why American culture is in decline. We will reference European culture to show the direction our own culture is heading. *American culture* refers to United States culture.

At this point in our decline the evidence is still unfolding and much of it is anecdotal but it provides excellent points for discussion. What is clear is that we continue to decline as we move further and further away from the nation's foundational principles: Judeo-Christian values, limited government, self-reliance and the Free Market system. The aim of this book is to analyze this decline and retreat from our foundational principles. We are not going to propose any solutions because there aren't any. We are following the natural trajectory of democracy. What American decline in particular, and Western decline in general, shows us is that Democracy is a temporary event in world history, that we are coming to the end of the current historical epoch that began emerging approximately five hundred years ago. This book will propose an educated speculation at what will replace the current epoch.

We are not going to "laundry list" horror stories -- they would fill volumes. The book will provide examples but the emphasis here is on analysis rather than stories and statistics. In this Internet age, researchers can find statistics and "facts" to support *any* argument and much of what we see on the Internet is unreliable. I have verified examples I cite in this book from other sources. Readers will find the *narrative* portion of the book all too familiar; the *analysis* is what I hope to add to the discussion of cultural decline.

I use the term *Secular Progressive* in lieu of *Liberal* since Secular Progressivism is the absolute corruption of Classical Liberalism. Secular Progressivism destroyed the legacy of Classical Liberalism.

This book is written from a conservative viewpoint. Secular Progressives will not agree with much of my analysis since the book places most of the blame for cultural decline both in the United States and Europe squarely on the Secular Progressive philosophy.

I avoid the use of hyphenated ethnicities such as *African-American* since these are divisive. White folks aren't European-Americans; neither are Blacks African-Americans. We are ALL Americans -- period.. A Native American is ANYONE who is born here; although anthropologically incorrect, the *t*erm *Inidan* or *American Indian* has validity through historical precedence,

I add the "personal touch" to the book using examples from my own experiences and those of my family.

Tom Reidy
Tacoma, WA
September 8, 2015

Contents

Chapter 1

Defining Culture

Before we begin our analysis of American cultural decline we need to define what a *culture* is and what it is built upon. There is nothing special or sacred about "culture**." Culture is simply *whatever works for a given people in a given place at a given time*.** No more, no less.

In addition to their own unique foundational principles, all cultures and societies are built on six pillars:

Political

Military

Economic

Intellectual

Moral (Religious)

Linguistic

(AUTHOR'S NOTE: I began my theory of culture in my book *Critical Mass: a chronicle of the American Catholic Church in the first generation after Vatican II*. At that time I introduced the first five pillars but have since added the sixth: Linguistic.)

For any culture to survive, these six pillars must remain intact and solid. When they are compromised they start to *weaken*, then *crumble*, then *collapse.* When they finally collapse they take the whole culture down with them. We will detail how this scenario of weakening, crumbling, and eventual collapse is occurring as of this writing (2015). We began the *weakening* stage in the 1960s. The *crumbling* began in the 1970s and the combination of global political, economic and military events in the first decade and a half of the 21st century makes the collapse of those pillars all but inevitable. The intellectual, moral and linguistic pillars have, for all intents and purposes, already collapsed.

Chapter 2

What Made American Culture Unique

The American Revolution could have gone the same direction as the French Revolution since the originators of both were products of the 18th century Enlightenment. When France overthrew King Louis XVI, it quickly turned into a dictatorship with thousands of executions of presumed "Enemies of the State." Eventually some of its leaders themselves (Robespierre, Danton) were executed. Within a few years the dictatorship was consolidated under Napoleon Bonaparte who made himself Emperor of France.

The United States did not go that route. During the American Revolution approximately one-third of the colonists remained loyal to England and King George III; another third remained neutral taking no side. That means only one-third of the American colonists supported the Revolution. After the American victory there were no executions of the other two-thirds. The Founding Fathers provided for a system of elected officials and drafted a constitution that was concise and specific in its enshrinement of certain "inalienable rights." The United States started out committed to limited government, personal opportunity and self-reliance based on Free Market economics.

Self-reliance was a relatively new concept at the time of the American Revolution. Self-reliance came out of the Protestant Reformation. Prior to the Reformation many Europeans were employed by the Catholic Church, chiefly the monasteries that supported themselves through farming and vineyards. The monasteries employed large numbers of peasants to run these operations. The Church had a tradition of taking care of people dating back to apostolic times when the early Christians lived in communities, pooled their resources and took care of one another. It was literally "small c" communism but in a good and positive -- and even holy -- sense. That tradition expanded through the Middle Ages in the monastic system that needed and employed laborers all across Europe. The Protestant Reformation dissolved the monasteries in the countries that broke away from the Catholic Church in favor of reformed doctrine. At least reformed doctrine was the official reason. The monasteries were huge landholdings and those monarchs who broke away from Rome seized Church lands for their own use and to buy favor from their nobility. Sweden had the wealthiest monastic system in Europe so it was no coincidence that it was the first European nation to accept Lutheranism (1523 -- but the final and official break with Rome occurred in 1536 when Canon Law was abolished in Sweden by Gustavus Vasa). England, with its own wealthy monastic system, followed the same course in 1534. This happened throughout Scandinavia and to a large extent in Germany as various German states opted for the Reformation.

The result was thousands of unemployed peasants. This gave rise to what became known as "The Protestant Ethic" which taught that you had to work hard and practice thrift since you could depend only on yourself and God. In other words, *it's all up to you*. No one is going to take care of you, not the Church and certainly not the government. The Founding Fathers slightly mitigated this harsh prescription by offering **opportunity** as in the guarantee of "life, liberty, and the *pursuit* of happiness." Not the guarantee of happiness; rather, the **pursuit** of happiness (opportunity). The United States will give you the opportunity to succeed by giving you plenty of freedom (not restricting you with myriads of laws, regulations and high taxes) built on a solid Free Market foundation. This lured millions of immigrants to the United States during the remainder of the 18th century, throughout the 19th and well into the 20th century, mostly from Europe where there was religious persecution and widespread poverty. The Protestant Ethic wasn't working too well over there since there were few *opportunities*. England, for instance, had a class system that was virtually impossible to rise out of. If you were a poor working man you were most likely going to stay a poor working man. In the United States you were not trapped into a poor class. You could come over here with nothing and eventually become a millionaire. Many did just that.

So America was unique in that regard (the only country in the world at that time with such a system) and was a magnet drawing millions away from Europe and more than a few from Asia as time went on.

It wasn't all perfect. We had Black slavery in the south, our national policy toward American Indians was too often unjust, and there was heavy discrimination against Roman Catholics although the later was never sanctioned by the government and numerous Catholics prospered in spite of it, including my own family. My grandfather had a good job with the Baltimore & Ohio Railroad in Akron, Ohio but in 1921 the Ku Klux Klan burned four crosses in a vacant lot across from my grandparents' house -- one cross for each Catholic family on the block. But this sort of thing never prevented Catholics and others from advancing. Even in the south there were prosperous Blacks. The first female self-made millionaire in the United States was a southern Black woman, Madame C.J. Walker (born Sarah Breedlove -- 1867-1919) who made her fortune in the hair care product industry. This could have only happened in the United States.

Chapter 3

The Six Cultural Pillars American Style

Let's take a look at the six cultural pillars and how they related to the United States. Note -- I say *related* (past tense) since we are currently in the crumbling stage. We are going to see what the pillars were like when they were solid and what they have sadly become.

Political

We were founded as a Republic with a strong constitution that guaranteed certain rights that were unknown in Europe and everywhere else at the time -- freedoms of speech, press, religion, and the right to bear arms as private citizens. While we did not have Universal Suffrage until 1920 and did not even have Universal (white) male suffrage until the 1830s, we still had an elected form of government.(**AUTHOR'S NOTE: Senators at the Federal Level were appointed at the state level until the passage of the 17th Amendment in 1913 that allowed for popular senatorial elections.**) The Separation of Powers as defined by the Constitution prevented coups, military takeovers, and other forms of upheaval that led to dictatorship. The Separation of Powers limited the control of the president thereby preventing an "imperial presidency." We had a two-party system presenting two different philosophies within the framework and intent of the Constitution. Third partiers occasionally sprang up but they were ineffective and short lived. When there are more than two parties you do not get an over 50 percent majority in national elections thus creating squabbling political parties that accomplish nothing. We saw an example of that in the 1992 and 1996 elections when we had three candidates and no one achieved a 50 percent plus plurality in either election. In those two elections the third party candidate, H. Ross Perot, did not have a party apparatus behind him but ran as an independent.

Historically, until the 1960s, there were not many differences between the two parties, Republican and Democrat. Republicans and Democrats both shared and supported traditional American values. Both were strong advocates of national defense. (President Kennedy, a

Democrat, wanted to close "The Missile Gap" between the United States and the Soviet Union in the early 1960s.) There were no major social issues such as abortion and same sex marriage dividing them. The Democrats favored more social spending but until the late 1960s neither party was "Entitlement based." That changed with President Lyndon Johnson's *Great Society* program, launched in 1965. It has mushroomed into an ever increasing Entitlement cornucopia. We had Public Assistance programs since 1935 when President Roosevelt enacted Social Security, Unemployment Insurance and Aid to Families with Dependent Children (AFDC). The first two required both employees and employers to pay into them. AFDC was designed for widows and orphans who were genuinely destitute. Social workers paid regular visits to AFDC households to ensure that recipients were not living beyond their means. No one was "entitled."

Since the late 1960s, divisions between the two parties have become sharply defined. Democrats are no longer pro-defense, actively opposing any kind of military action and are constantly cutting the Defense budget when they are in power. As of now, we are facing a major and growing threat from the Islamic State of Iraq and Syria (ISIS) that has already taken over large parts of Iraq and Syria and is now entrenched in Libya. We have willing allies in Egypt and Jordan, the Kurdish Peshmerga and, of course, Israel, and could easily destroy ISIS but the Democrats refuse to support any kind of military action beyond token and largely ineffective air strikes while the Republicans are ready to do whatever it takes to defeat ISIS.

The Democrats have turned against Israel, our most reliable ally in the Middle East. Until recently the Democrats were staunchly pro-Israel but now favor the Palestinians. The Democratic Party is now totally controlled by its Secular Progressive base that opposes Israel and supports the Palestinians. The Republicans are strongly pro-Israel. Democrats see the Palestinians as "victims" of Israeli expansion conveniently ignoring the thousands of rockets that Hamas, the elected government of the Palestinian Authority, periodically uses to attack Israel but scolds Israel for retaliating while ignoring the efforts Israel takes to avoid excessive collateral damage.

(AUTHOR'S NOTE: I included that somewhat lengthy comment on Israel since it underscores a dangerous cultural trend that we will explore in more depth in our discussion of Multiculturalism.)

Iran has sworn to destroy both Israel and the United States but the Democratic Administration of President Barack Obama has negotiated a treaty with Iran that is supposed to stop them from acquiring nuclear weapons. The treaty will at best delay Iranian production of nuclear weapons and does not prevent Iran from building missile delivery systems. Iran does not want no notice inspection or compliance verification and is demanding the lifting of all sanctions and release of all frozen Iranian financial assets -- money that was frozen as a result of the 1979 Iranian takeover of the U.S. Embassy in Tehran and holding Embassy personnel hostage for 444 days. The Administration lifted many of the sanctions and unfrozen some of the money before the treaty was finalized. This treaty will have the whole world rushing in to do business with Iran and surging its economy. This is a major strategic political defeat for the United States -- and Israel.

Democrats favor a European social democratic form of government. Since 2009 an increasing number of Americans are receiving government Entitlements (Food Stamps, Medicaid etc.). A Google search revealed that 46, 674,364 Americans currently receive Food Stamps. According to the Henry J. Kaiser Family Foundation, 70 million Americans are receiving Medicaid in 2015. With the enactment of the Affordable healthcare Act (Obamacare) the Federal Government took over the American Healthcare industry which amounts to 16 percent of the United States economy. The Affordable Healthcare Act was enacted March 28, 2010 and much of the law was phased in by January 2014. The Law will be completely implemented by 2020. The Federal Government now dictates to health insurance companies what they must include in their coverage which is often more than the patient needs or wants but has to pay for in much higher premiums, co-pays, deductibles and out of pocket expenses.

The Democrats refuse to do anything about our porous southern border while Republicans want to secure it with a high tech fence. Republicans, for the most part, are pro-life, support traditional marriage and do not believe in physician assisted suicide and legalized drugs while the Democratic Party actively supports these positions. The Democratic policies favor Big Government, Entitlement and a European economic model which is essentially Socialist.

These divisions have caused political gridlock which makes it impossible to develop meaningful legislation and solutions to an ever increasing number of national problems that will permanently undermine the country if they are not resolved. The Affordable Healthcare Act was passed when Democrats controlled the White House, the Senate and House of Representatives. Not one Republican voted for it. President Obama has used gridlock as an excuse to sign numerous Executive Orders that may be unconstitutional such as "temporarily" legalizing five million illegal immigrants allowing them to remain in the United States. He is usurping authority the Constitution gives to Congress alone. He is trying to do the same with the Iran nuclear treaty by going around the Senate and taking it to the United Nations. The Constitution states that the Senate must approve treaties with a two-thirds majority. By taking it directly to the UN, he gets international approval thereby isolating the Senate. The Supreme Court's legalization of same sex marriage was in clear violation of the 10th Amendment as we shall see later.

Entitlements destroy self-reliance. According to the U.S. Census Bureau 49.2 percent of American households received some kind of Government payment in 2011-- that's 151 million people out of a population of 306.8 million. This includes Social Security and Medicare with millions being added to those programs every year so the percentage will remain constant. One-third receive means tested Entitlements. Whether they are working or earned their Entitlements from past employment, or are poor, they are nevertheless *dependent* on government.

Big Government is all about control and the quickest way to control is to create dependency and a dependent society is a weak society vulnerable to external conquest and internal dictatorship. Dependency saps will, creativity and initiative. What has Europe contributed to the world in the past 70 years?

Here is a recent development to underscore how dependent we have become on Entitlements. Seattle is raising the minimum wage to $15.00 per hour. A local television news program reported that some employees are asking for fewer hours because the increase in their wages will adversely affect their government benefits -- subsidized housing, subsidized daycare and Food Stamps. Amounts of these benefits would be reduced. They are not celebrating an upward path out of dependency; they are resisting it because they have become addicted to dependency.

Limited government and self-reliance were the solid oak and granite that formed the political pillar and held it together. Entitlements, divisive social issues, and polar opposite political philosophies based on conflicting values (Traditional vs Secular Progressive) are the jackhammers that are crumbling this pillar. None of these forces were in play before the mid-1960s. This pillar has basically collapsed. Republicans represent an America that is rapidly fading away as we shall see as this book unfolds. The Democrats have no philosophy having become a "bread and circuses" party pandering to the demands (many of them outrageous) of various constituencies in return for votes.

Military

The Military has become a political football since the 1960s. Republicans build it up and Democrats tear it down through drastic cuts in personnel, resources and funding. We are rapidly approaching the lowest troop levels since World War II. We still have the best military technology (weapons systems, ships and aircraft) but in other ways we are behind the times. The face of war is changing. The military needs to develop "in and out" strategies that utilize Special Ops, Delta Force and Navy SEAL Teams. In my book *New Paradigms*, I make the case for a 50,000 man elite force that would meet the needs of 21st century warfare across the globe. Defense of the American homeland would be handled by an expanded and updated Federal National Guard.

The decline in the U.S. Military is defined in its failure to develop and implement the new style of warfare we need tp successfully defeat ISIS and other terrorist groups in various parts of the world. It's a classic example of that old expression, "the generals are always fighting the last war" but the politicians share the blame as well since they are the people in charge and refuse to give the military the go ahead to accomplish this goal. At home we need to locate military installations according to national security requirements, not where they will provide the most economic benefit to a regional economy. We are currently stuck in a 20th century paradigm. We need to create one force to meet overseas contingencies and another specializing in homeland defense. The military pillar has not reached the crumbling stage but it is in a weakened condition in relation to 21st century warfare strategy. The prospects for needed change are slim as long as the military is a political hostage.

Economic

The American economy was built on the Free Market system. Anyone could start a business or a farm with a minimum of government regulations and taxation. The Personal Income tax was not instituted until 1913.

The Free Market system coupled with limited government (minimal taxation and regulation) created opportunities that led to innovation unequaled by any other country. A partial list of our inventors includes Eli Whitney (the cotton gin), Elias Howe (sewing machine), Samuel Morse (telegraph), Alexander Graham Bell (the telephone), Thomas Edison (the phonograph and the electric light bulb), the Wright Brothers (the airplane), and Philo Farnsworth (television). The United States pioneered the automobile and airplane industries making them what they are today both at home and overseas. The modern computer and electronics industries owe their genesis to the American genius of Bill Gates and Steve Jobs.

The three great drivers of the American economy were the thousands of small farms, small businesses, and factories that dotted the American landscape and created a strong middle class which enabled national self-sufficiency. These drivers are now gone. Agribusiness destroyed the small farms, mega businesses and box stores destroyed the small neighborhood businesses (e.g., mom and pop grocery stores and hardware stores) while heavy handed government regulations and taxation (The United States has the highest corporate tax rate in the world) drove American industry offshore. We now import almost everything, much of it from China to whom we are now a debtor nation. What we do make here (computers and airplanes) is made from imported parts. Customer service phone calls are handled by citizens of India and the

Philippines. As the average American citizen is increasingly dependent on government, the American economy is dependent on foreign countries some of whom are openly hostile to America and its national interests.

The Bottom Line is the National Debt which currently exceeds $18 trillion. Fifty years ago, in 1965, the National Debt was $317 billion. Since 2009 the National Debt has increased by over one trillion dollars per year; much of this is due to Entitlement spending. According to the Heritage Foundation, the 2015 Federal budget allocates 11 percent for Welfare and other Entitlement programs, 24 [percent for Social Security payments, and 25 percent for Medicare, Medicaid and other healthcare programs. That equals 60 percent of the annual Federal budget.

The U.S. dollar is the world's strongest currency but only by default. It is an illusion since the dollar has had no standard of measurement since President Nixon took it off the Gold Standard in 1971 for the purpose of achieving short term economic gains that would pay off in the 1972 elections. The dollar, like the British Pound did for so many years, is living on its past. The only way to stimulate the economy in its present state is to print money and the government did this through "Quantitative Easing" which, at its height, was printing $85 billion every month giving a false impression of prosperity since it drove the Stock Market to record levels.

The economic pillar has virtually collapsed. We can only rescue the economy by reducing Entitlement spending and enacting a "Manhattan style" re-industrialization effort. Re-industrialization would require a massive reduction in government regulations (including environmental regulations) and tax breaks along with restraining powerful labor unions. For a project of this magnitude, government loans and subsidies would be necessary and some of that would have to come out of the Entitlement budget.

The National Debt crisis will need some out of the box thinking (paying foreign creditors in oil, natural gas and other commodities and tax breaks for domestic creditors until they equal full payment) since we will never pay off $18 trillion in the conventional manner. The Democrats will not do this and the Republicans lack the will to fight for it. The economic pillar is too closely tied into our political pillar and we have already seen what kind of shape we are in there.

Intellectual

We have produced a body of literature equal to any European literary tradition. Henry Thoreau, Herman Melville, Edgar Allan Poe, Nathaniel Hawthorne, Henry Wadsworth Longfellow, Mark Twain, Washington Irving, Ralph Waldo Emerson, and Emily Dickinson were just a few of the 19th century greats. The 20th century included Gertrude Stein, Ernest Hemmingway, F. Scott Fitzgerald, William Faulkner, Sinclair Lewis, Ayn Rand, John Updike, and Edna Ferber, and more.

The United States topped the motion picture industry with classics like *Casablanca*, *It's a Wonderful Life*, *Double Indemnity*, *Citizen Kane*, *Ben-Hur*, A *Tree Grows in Brooklyn*, *The Ten Commandments*, *The Robe*, *Demetrius and the Gladiators,* to name just a very few plus a series of unparalleled musicals -- *South Pacific*, *Guys and Dolls*, *Oklahoma*, *Carousel*, *The Flower Drum Song*, *West Side Story*, and *The Sound of Music*.

The stars of this motion picture era known as "The Golden Age of Hollywood" are still embedded in the national psyche: James Stewart, Orson Wells, Donna Reed, Katherine Hepburn, Spencer Tracy, Cary Grant, Charlton Heston, Clark Gable, Elizabeth Taylor, Victor Mature, Bette Davis, Joan Crawford, Bing Crosby, Bob Hope, Jimmy Cagney and John Wayne -- just to name some of them. Contemporary "celebrities" will never achieve that kind of icon status because they will not stand the test of time like the above mentioned do. The culture of that period was more conducive and therefore better able to produce talent of that brilliance. The culture today is too diminished to accomplish that.

And we cannot omit the great television personalities of the 1940s up through the 1960s -- Ed Sullivan, Steve Allen, Lucille Ball, Joan Davis, Milton Berle, Bishop Sheen, George Gobel, Jackie Gleason, Sid Caesar, Martha Raye, and Johnny Carson -- again, to name just a few. Television followed a great radio tradition, much of which spilled over into television -- *The Great Gildersleeve, Fibber McGee and Molly, Our Miss Brooks, Mister District Attorney. Mr. and Mrs. North, The Whistler,* and many others.

We had a brilliant musical tradition; composers -- George Gershwin, Irving Berlin and Cole Porter; singers of the caliber of Frank Sinatra, Kate Smith, Mario Lanza and Bing Crosby; the Big Band era from the 1930s through the 1950s; the greatest pianists of the 20th century, Liberace and Oscar Levant; the Do-op music tradition of the late 1950s and early 1960s is still widely listened to and many of that genre's singers are still well known -- Jay and the Americans, The Everly Brothers, Buddy Holly. Roy Orbison, Lesley Gore and many others. This musical era produced the greatest singing talent in American history -- Elvis Presley. (Some would award that honor to Frank Sinatra.)

Today the music industry is dominated by Rap and Hip Hop that make liberal use of four letter words along with racial and gender slurs. As I was walking home one evening I heard a boom box, at least a block away, reverberating "F*** that s***, f*** that s***, f*** that s***..." multiple times. On another occasion, I passed a car waiting for a light and the CD player in the car was screaming "N*****s talkin' s***, n*****s talkin' s***, n*****s talkin' s***..."

Few movies are noteworthy and while we have a few good actors and singers out there, none of them have the lasting impact of those listed above. What we have are a lot of so-called "celebrities" who are more famous for the trouble they get into than the "talent" they present. "Personalities" such as Justin Bieber, Lindsey Lohan, Brittany Spears, Miley Cyrus and Paris Hilton are low on talent but high on notoriety for the problems in their personal lives. These people focus on being outrageous and controversial -- not creating genuine lasting art. Kim Kardashian is simply famous for being famous; famous for what is a mystery. She has accomplished nothing but her name is always out there.

On the academic level we are home to some of the best colleges and universities in the world -- Harvard, Yale, Princeton, Dartmouth, The Massachusetts Institute of Technology, Harvey Mudd College of Engineering, and great teaching hospitals like the University of Washington and UCLA. In addition, we had a great Public School system that provided a solid education even if it had to be backed up by the hack paddle on occasion. Public education has been on a downhill trajectory since the mid-1960s that was documented at length in the 1984 report *A*

Nation at Risk. We are at the bottom rung of the industrialized world in math and science (which explains why we are importing so many physicians, engineers, computer techs and other technical expertise). If you watch certain television shows like the old Jay Leno *Jaywalking* segments and Watters World on *The O'Reilly Factor,* you will regularly see young people (the Millennial generation) who know absolutely nothing about American history and current events. College students cannot answer simple questions like who did we fight in World War II ("France?"); who won the Civil War? ("We did."); what year was the Declaration of Independence signed? ("1964"); who is the vice-president? ("Uhhhh…"). I admit that this is all anecdotal but this happens all the time on these segments. Millennials on the quiz show *Name the Celebrity* can name current pop stars and contemporary celebrities but have no idea about older personalities. One of them identified Fidel Castro as a singer. I suggest you ask young people these types of questions and see what kind of answers you get.

There is no greater indication of cultural decline than the members of a society lacking the cultural literacy to pass their culture on to future generations.

We have lost our culture of literature, music and entertainment. Some will argue that what we have today is just as solid -- only "different." What is lacking in today's literature, movies, television and music? The answer to that question is ***Cultural Maturity***. What makes today's entertainment, writing and music ***culturally immature*** is that they pander to the lowest common denominator of the culture -- society's baser inclinations. The old literature, movies, television and music appealed to a higher sense. If you keep this concept in mind when you watch a movie, read a book or listen to contemporary music, you will understand. We have become so dumbed down in our intellectual tradition over so many years that we have become culturally numb and blind.

Moral/Religious

The United States was founded on Judeo-Christian principles; throughout most of our history we observed and practiced a strict and exact moral code. Being a divorced man was a factor in Adlai Stevenson losing the presidential elections in 1952 and 1956. The reason why we had a low crime rate during the Great Depression was a well-defined sense of morality and a work ethic: you could always eat if you could pick up a broom. During the Depression, when hobos would come up from the Akron rail yards looking for a meal in exchange for work, my grandmother would give them some work to do and then give them a good meal when they had finished the job. They worked. They didn't steal and rape. It was a reflection of a strong work ethic and a strong sense of morality. Television programs like *Little House on the Prairie* and *The Waltons* were accurate portrayals of that America.

We expected our politicians to be honest while Europeans laughed at us when we were shocked by the Watergate scandal in 1972-74. Martha Mitchell, wife of Attorney-General John Mitchell, summed it up in her shock and surprised laced remark: "Mister President lied to us." Europeans just accepted lying and corrupt politicians as natural. Americans did not -- then. I remember my aunt remarking during a conversation back in the early 1960s: "Well, if you can't trust the government, who can you trust?" Today such a comment would be considered naiveté and gullibility on steroids.

Americans were a deeply religious people with movies and television reflecting the religious nature of the culture. The 1950s and early 1960s produced numerous religious movies -- *Samson and Delilah, The Robe, Demetrius and the Gladiators, Quo Vadis, The Ten Commandments, King of Kings, The Greatest Stiory Ever Told* -- while Bishop Sheen edged out Milton Berle ("Mr. Television") in the mid-1950s when they aired in the same time slot on different networks. Spencer Tracy and Bing Crosby looked more like priests than the ordained clergy did in their motion picture portrayals -- Tracy as Fr. Flannigan in *Boys Town* and Crosby as Fr. O'Malley in *Going My Way* and *The Bells of St. Mary's*.

The entertainment industry is a reflection of the American culture and it, at one , reflected a deeply moral and religious society. Look at the movies and television programs of today. They are a reflection of what our culture has become. I don't think that needs any elaboration. Contemporary movies and television are based on sexual innuendo and, much of the time, sex -- period. While there is some good viewing on the news channels, the Discovery Channel, the History Channel, the National Geographic Channel and a few others, it is clear that the entertainment component of television has exhausted itself and this is painfully evident from those crazy "reality" shows that feature dysfunctional people making idiots out of themselves. Television, being the mirror of the culture, is simply reflecting a morally dysfunctional culture.

This pillar has all but crumbled into dust and much of the blame lies in the lap of the religious institutions. The churches are not providing leadership. This is clear from the number of churchgoers who have accepted abortion, same sex marriage, physician assisted suicide and legalized drugs as "the law of the land" and while they may not be totally comfortable with these evils, they are not going to actively oppose them. As the saying foes "Evil prevails when good people do nothing' and the churches and their congregations are doing a lot of nothing today. Only the churches that make moral demands on their members are seeing any increase while the "peace and love" churches are fading. We will talk more of this in our discussion of the disintegration of our foundational institutions.

Linguistic

English is the international language. It is the language of business, international diplomacy, technology, and the airlines industry (including air traffic control). This is all due to American influence -- not British influence. England has been on a downward trend since the end of World War I while the American influence began rising after World War I. English as the international language is the direct result of American political, military, economic, and intellectual influence throughout the world.

Today the Linguistic pillar is crumbling thanks to two sets of cultural termites. Multiculturalism, which we will discuss at length later, that is giving cultural equality to various foreign languages, especially Spanish. Government agencies and private corporations are spending huge amounts of money producing documentation in a growing plethora of languages destroying the incentive of immigrants to learn English. Anyone who suggests making English the Official Language is immediately labeled by Secular Progressives as racist, xenophobic and anti-immigrant.

Language is the unifying characteristic of any society. Multiple languages lead to fragmentation. Dual languages (English and French) almost led to the breakup of Canada into an English speaking country (Canada) and a French speaking country (Quebec). There were two referendums in Quebec regarding independence, one in 1980 and another in1995, and on both occasions the majority voted to remain part of Canada. Multiple languages is a leading factor in the ongoing chaos in India. It has caused problems in Belgium between speakers of Flemish and French.

The second cause of linguistic decay in the United States is the coarsening of the language. Another sign of educational decline is the inability of so many younger people to speak and write a coherent sentence indicating a lack of critical thinking skills. Their sentences are peppered with "like, "um, "see (or know) what I'm sayin' '' and "ya know." I was listening to a teen-age girl talk on her cell phone on the bus and I counted her using the word "like" 27 times in the course of one mile. People who cannot present themselves well verbally will have much greater difficulty in finding employment.

Worse yet, the language has become increasingly vulgar. Movies and music are overloaded with foul language including "F bombs" and "N bombs." You hear swearing and foul language all the time as you walk down the street. There is nothing new about that sort of language. It was primarily used when the guys -- and the gals -- got together in private. In the past it was rarely used in mixed company and less frequently in public. When I was in college I was sitting with two male friends and a girl who was a close friend of mine. She and I did use salty language when we were together. (Hey, it was the '60s.) During the course of the conversation I said "Oh, that's a bunch of s***." I was later reprimanded by my male friends for saying that word in front of a girl. That was in 1968. How times have changed. And it's not only young people; just recently I was sitting outside a Starbucks sipping an iced tea and a 40 something man walked by talking on his cell phone spewing out four letter words, one right after the other. More than occasionally I'll see someone (usually a male) walking down the street screaming out nothing but four letter words and other assorted bad language to no one in particular. These people are probably wasted on drugs. This usually happens in the downtown area. How is foul language source of cultural decline? It destroys personal respect, civil discourse and vastly increases the possibility of exploding into physical confrontation between people having an argument or disagreement. Many of these shootings that we hear about on the evening local news were escalations of what started out as verbal confrontation.

There are differences in the way English is spoken in Britain, Canada, the United States, Australia and New Zealand. Britain often uses words in a different way than we do: the hood of a car is the *bonnet*, the trunk is the *boot* and a truck is a *lorry*. I was making a telephone call in England and the operator informed me that "The exchange is engaged." "Oh, the line's busy," I replied. Australia has a complex and sophisticated (for want of a better word) slang. Spelling may vary e.g., British English reverses the "e" and the "r": theatre (British) theater (American); centre (British) center (American). British English adds a "u" in certain words -- (e.g., harbour and honour.).

Ebonics aka African-American Vernacular English was offered as a subject in the Oakland, California school district and is considered by some as a dialect of English. Ebonics does away with the verbs *am, are* and *is* replacing them with *be*. "I am going to the store" becomes "I be going to the store." *Themselves* becomes *theyselves*. *Theirs* becomes *theys*. Ask becomes *axe* and asked translates to *axed*. Linguists can debate the value and legitimacy of Ebonics. It appears to have a history as a dialect but it has become more of a political and sociological dialect in the contemporary culture. Using Ebonics in a job interview guarantees non-selection.

If English becomes too coarsened, too reliant on words such as "like", and the use of Ebonics and other potential dialects becomes widespread, how long will English remain the international language? One of the reasons the motion picture and music industries have become so *culturally immature* is that they are using too much of that sort of degraded language. Dialects of any kind are degraded forms of the mother tongue. All languages have dialects and I do not use the word *degraded* in a negative way; rather, in the grammatical sense.

Linguistic decline as a cultural phenomenon traces its origin to the Free Speech Movement, one of the earliest incarnations of the Counterculture, in late 1964 at UC Berkeley. This amounted to little more than screaming foul language into microphones and megaphones but it was a sign of rebellion that could be easily utilized by the Hippie generation as a vehicle to reject their parents' values. Coarse and vulgar language became culturally acceptable in the 1960s. Males used it because it was "cool" and women did it to be "assertive." Today it has become common parlance and you hear it coming out of the mouths of kindergartners. It has also become the vernacular of the Millennials. This is one cultural pillar that is getting passed on in its corrupted and crumbled form.

Chapter 4

The Unraveling of American Culture

Before we look at cultural unravelling we need to put a date on when this trend began. We might not be able to pinpoint a day and a month but we can single out a specific year: **1966**.

Why 1966?

(1) The Sexual Revolution began in 1966.

(2) 1966 was the year that popular music became loud and harsh with often morbid themes; the opposite of the romantic, idyllic love celebrated in the Do-Op music of the late 1950s and early 1960s -- not to mention the Big band era of the 1930s up through the 1950s. Music is a major definer of culture.

(3) Drug use went viral in 1966 -- not only marijuana, but psychedelic drugs (LSD) along with heroin and cocaine. When I graduated from high school in 1964 marijuana wasn't on the cultural radar screen. In 1966 drug usage was rampant even in high schools.

(4) Race riots, anti-Vietnam anti-war demonstrations became violent while anarchist demonstrations were breaking out across Europe.

(5) Civility gave way to an "in your face" confrontational style learned from demonstrations and riots and encouraged because it seemed to get results.

(6) Authority was being questioned at every level -- the home, schools, churches, the work place, and the government.

(7) 1966 ushered in the era of mass shootings when Charles Whitman killed 14 and wounded 32 at the University of Texas in Austin, Texas on August 1, 1966. Before the killing spree at the University he killed his wife and mother bringing the total to 16 dead.

(8) Divorce and out-of-wedlock births became acceptable followed soon after by legalized abortion and open homosexuality. (**AUTHOR'S NOTE: In chapter 5 we will discuss the problems with homosexual activity at the societal and cultural levels rather than the moral/religious issues associated with it.**)

(9) Religious observance began declining in 1966 especially within mainstream Catholicism and Protestantism. There was a marked decline in Roman Catholic seminary entry classes in 1966 from the previous year.

(10) And, for what it's worth, Anton Sandor LaVey founded the First Church of Satan in San Francisco in 1966. He called 1966 "the Year Zero."

Most cultural paradigms take decades to evolve. This one came out of nowhere mostly in one single year.

None of the following bullet points would have been considered possible or even imaginable in the early 1960s (pre-1966).

- At least half of all marriages end in divorce. Most children in any given public school now come from what used to be known as a "broken home." The term du jour is "Fragmented Families" -- families with step-parents or headed by a single parent, usually a single mother.

- Approximately 57 million legal abortions since the Supreme Court legalized it on a nationwide basis in 1973. Since at least the 1980s the Democratic Party's presidential and vice-presidential nominees must be pro-choice (abortion).

- Widespread acceptance of homosexuality resulting in nationwide legalization of same sex marriage by the Supreme Court in June 2015. Same sex marriage is enshrined in the Democratic Party platform, along with abortion, as a civil right.

- Movies and television are saturated with sexual themes, foul language, and wanton violence that can only be described as sadistic and diabolical; until the early 1960s couples portraying married couples could not be shown in the same bed unless they were actually married in real life (e.g., Ozzie and Harriet Nelson). Toilets could not appear in bathroom scenes.

- Crime rates have skyrocketed. Today the majority of homes have burglar alarms. In the early 1960s, people felt safe leaving their doors unlocked. I never knocked when entering the home of one of my best friends from grade school and high school. I simply walked in. They left the backdoor unlocked during the day even if no one was home.

- Child abductions have increased. Children can no longer play safely outside or walk to school unescorted. Fifty years ago kindergarten children walked to school by themselves. I did. Today, parents can be charged with a criminal offense if they allow children that age to go anywhere by themselves. Many of these abductions are perpetrated by the non-custodial parents involved in messy divorces and child custody battles, but many are carried out by sexual deviants. Every week there is at least on story on the news about someone trying to lure a child into his car. You can go on line and find out how many registered sex offenders are living in your neighborhood. Large cities have thousands of them.

- Churches, school districts, sports teams -- any organization where young people are involved -- have been torn apart by sex abuse and pedophilia scandals.

- Domestic violence has reached pandemic proportions. Domestic violence has always been around but in the past, the strong societal moral code governing male conduct toward women prevented much of it. Today those standards are gone and the abuse rate has increased accordingly. Much domestic violence is committed by young men who grew up with no positive male role models in their lives and, consequently, do not know how to act like real men. Drugs and alcohol are strong contributors to domestic violence as well.

- Homelessness has been increasing exponentially. It is no longer confined to hobos in rail yards. Mental illness, drug abuse and the disintegration of the once strong American family unit have all contributed to this; previously, mental patients were in hospitals, drug abuse was minimal and families took better care of one another.

- Mass shootings are becoming more and more commonplace where shooters kill as many people as possible then commit suicide. Shootings in schools are almost always done by students at the school where they carry out their crimes. The two worst shootings were at Columbine High School in Columbine, Colorado (April 20, 1999) where two students killed 12 other students and one teacher and wounded 21 others before committing suicide; and Virginia Polytechnic Institute and State University in Blacksburg, Virginia on April 16, 2007 where one student killed 32 and wounded 17 before killing himself. There have been many more school shootings with smaller numbers of fatalities and many more that were stopped before they took place.

Mass killings: The Tate-LaBianca murders in Los Angeles (August 9-10, 1969) where 7 victims including rising film star Sharon Tate and her 8 month unborn baby on August 9th by the notorious "Manson Family" Hippie commune. The following day the Manson Family murdered supermarket executive Leno LaBianca and his wife, Rosemary, in their home; Jonestown, Guyana (November 18, 1978) with the mass suicide of 918 people at the direction of cult leader Jim Jones; Aurora, CO theater massacre (July 20, 2012) 12 killed and 58 injured; Sandy Hook

Elementary school in Newtown, CT (Dec.14, 2012) 26 killed, most of them first graders. The theater shooter was captured by police and the Sandyhook killer committed suicide.

There are increasing incidences of work place violence as angry ex-employees act out their rage by shooting co-workers and bosses.

- We are no longer an economic superpower. Since 1966 our industrial base has withered as more and more jobs are outsourced to foreign countries and what we do manufacture here is often done with outsourced parts imported from overseas.

- Most families now need two incomes to survive as the economy grows increasingly uncertain. Layoffs have become common since the 1960s and very few people work for the same company as a lifetime career -- a commonplace event up until the early 1960s. Most people change jobs and careers on a regular basis just to survive.

- A National Debt of more than $18 trillion.

- A constant feeling of anxiety and uncertainty about the future. Contrast that to the "Camelot era" of the Kennedy Administration (1961 - 63) when national optimism was at an all-time high.

We cannot whitewash our pre-1966 history.   We had slavery, the Civil War, the Great Depression and institutionalized racism in the South with its segregation and Jim Crow Laws. No society is perfect. The difference is that we eventually resolved these problems on our own. The bullet points detailed in this chapter are not only unresolved but may have reached the point where, in all probability, they have no resolution.

Chapter 5

Cultural "Choke Points"

In this chapter we are going to look at 20 cultural "choke points" that have contributed to cultural decline in the United States. Each one of these is a topic for a book in itself but we will summarize them in a way sufficient to understand why they have contributed to cultural decline.

1. ***The United States creates government enacted Public Assistance: Welfare (Aid to Families with Dependent Children), Social Security and Unemployment Insurance. (1935)***

While well intentioned and designed to give Americans some relief from the Great Depression, take care of widows and orphans and provide income during periods of unemployment and an old age pension, these programs planted the seeds of the "Entitlement mentality" that dominates American society today and is killing the American bedrock foundation of self-reliance and limited government. Over the ensuing years and decades, government Entitlements have vastly expanded generating an ever increasing dependence on government. Today approximately 60 percent of the American public receives some kind of government Entitlement. The Federal Government subsidizes most State Entitlement programs. If there ever was a "slippery slope", the 1935 Public Assistance legislation is it.

Let's take a look at each one of these programs.

Aid to Families with Dependernt Children

This was originally intended to support widows and orphans when first signed into law. Requirements were strict and recipients were monitored to ensure they were not living beyond their means. President Lyndon Johnson greatly expanded this program in the late 1960s with *The Great Society* Program. It soon ended up supporting families headed primarily by unwed single mothers. The illegitimacy rate skyrocketed. Today out-of-wedlock births among the Black community are at 72 percent and the Hispanic Community is at 53 percent. Whites are around 30 percent and the overall national out-of-wedlock birth rate is around 40 percent. It was 6 percent in 1960. The Black family unit was the most solid in the country before The Great Society greatly expanded AFDC. The Hispanics also had a strong family unit but easy access to Entitlements made it easy for the "fathers" to abandon their responsibilities and unwed mothers found that they got a "raise" with each new child.

(AUTHOR'S NOTE: Welfare is only one cause of family breakdown in the United States. The Sexual Revolution (see below) is the major driver.)

Welfare has become generational as children growing up in that system learn how to manipulate it and stay on board. AFDC -- known since 1996 as Temporary Assistance for Needy Families (TANF) comes with Food Stamps and free medical insurance (Medicaid). In many cases, Welfare recipients qualify for subsidized public housing and state paid childcare. It has reached the point where many Welfare recipients would take a "pay cut" (when you include the entire package of benefits) if they took a job, part time or full time. When I worked for the State of Washington Department of Employment Security (Workfirst unit) I knew people who would find good paying jobs, get off Welfare, and then come back on because they were psychologically conditioned to receiving *guaranteed* Welfare benefits every month. Sure, it wasn't nearly as much as the job paid but it was *guaranteed* -- they did not have to meet an employer's demands and expectations and they didn't have to worry about getting "laid off" from Welfare. Work made them ineligible for other benefits that came with the Welfare payment.   This mindset directly contradicts the Founders' intentions of creating *opportunities* ("the pursuit of happiness" -- opportunities to gain wealth) and not guarantees.

The Welfare Reform Act of 1996 did place a 60 month lifetime limit on cash assistance but while they were in that timeframe they were *guaranteed* a *secure* income that included Food Stamps, Medicaid, and other benefits. The only time limit was on cash assistance -- Food Stamps, Medicaid and Housing had no time limit. (From 2002-2011 Washington State allowed TANF recipients to receive monthly cash assistance indefinitely beyond 60 months and the Welfare Reform Act itself allows for indefinite extensions of cash assistance on a case-by-case basis for up to 20 percent of the individual State's caseload.)   The State may put them in the

Workfirst Program meaning they had to look for work but there were other activities they could pursue to meet the requirements of the Workfirst program such as going to school and enrolling in job training programs which many Welfare recipients did. The predecessor programs to the Welfare Reform Act of 1996 had no time limits for cash assistance and plenty of opportunities for school including, in some cases, free college degrees. The Welfare Reform Act eliminated four year college degrees and the ability to stay on cash assistance for life but while recipients were on TANF there were a lot of programs and benefits available to them. If recipients did not comply with Workfirst requirements they could be "sanctioned" with loss of a percentage of their monthly cash payment but all they had to do was promise to play ball and they were back to the full grant.

Welfare never paid more cash than necessary to pay for rent and utilities but many recipients work "under the table", received money from relatives or lived with someone who contributed to their support. Many Welfare recipients I worked with had top of the line cable TV packages. Many smoked and others were regulars at casinos prompting the state to ban Welfare recipients from cashing their Electronic Benefit Transfer (EBT) cards at gambling establishments. The State no longer makes home visits unless there is strong evidence of fraud and other kinds of abuse.

Welfare, once a stigma, is now a culture unto itself. I recommend *Framework for Understanding Poverty* by Ruby Payne, Ph.D as an excellent study in generational poverty.

Social Security

Social Security began as an old age pension. It was intended to pay senior citizens and would be financed by the payroll tax levied on working Americans. People supported this and did not mind paying because it would be there for them when they retired. But over time it expanded into a lot more. It pays disability insurance to those physically or mentally unable to work. Originally, a recipient had to first pay into it for a certain number of quarters to be eligible to receive disability payments but later Social Security became the financier of Supplemental

Security Income (SSI) which is basically a welfare program because you do not have to pay anything into it to receive benefits.

Social Security pays survivor benefits to children of deceased beneficiaries (including those who die before reaching the minimum age to receive Social Security) until they are 18. Ex-spouses can draw on a payee's benefits if they were married for more than ten years and if their own Social Security payment would be less than half the payee's or if these spouses had never paid into Social Security. This means that an unlimited number of people can draw off ne payee's benefits if they meet eligibility requirements.

The Federal Government has routinely raided the Social Security Trust Fund to finance other projects. This practice dates back to the Johnson Administration (1963-1968). Many people now rely on Social Security as their only retirement income. It was originally intended as a *supplement*. When Social Security was signed into law in 1935 most elderly people would live out their last years with other family members so there would not be total dependence on the system. At this point in our national evolution it has made senior citizens a dependent (on the government) class since the vast majority of them could not survive without Social Security.

Unemployment Insurance

Different states pay different amounts of Unemployment Insurance. What you receive is based on how much you earned and you must have worked a specified number of hours during a specified number of quarters. In Washington State, Unemployment Insurance "premiums" are entirely paid for through a tax on the employer. The individual state decides if you qualify. A lay off (lack of work) will normally qualify you for benefits as will many reasons for getting fired other than misconduct. Quits are adjudicated more strenuously. The normal period for drawing Unemployment Insurance is 26 weeks but after the 2008 recession it was extended to 99 weeks with the Federal Government paying most of the freight beyond the first 26 weeks. Federal and state extensions are usually offered during times of economic downturn.

Having worked as Unemployment claims taker, I saw many cases of recipient malfeasance such as turning in "padded" job search logs. Washington State requires only three employer contacts per week while paying a maximum of $604.00 per week. This makes Unemployment Insurance attractive and, if a spouse is working or the person is living at home with parents, there is less incentive to find work. Training and schooling are also available while a person is drawing Unemployment under the Trade Act so that makes staying on Unemployment Insurance even more attractive.

All that being said, most people on Unemployment Insurance are genuinely looking for work but more than a few are not. Free money becomes habit forming. It's human nature especially when Unemployment recipients may be eligible for Food Stamps, Medicaid, or other benefits while collecting Unemployment Insurance. Many people will hold out to the last minute before taking a job that pays less than their Unemployment.

Conclusion

What made AFDC, Social Security and Unemployment Insurance a cultural choke point is that these programs started us on the road to becoming an Entitlement based and dependent society moving us away from self-reliance and limited government since it takes Big Government to maintain an Entitlement based society. Limited government is by definition small government. These three original programs created a domino effect begetting Food Stamps, Medicare/Medicaid, subsidized public housing, government paid training programs, government paid childcare, Pell grants to finance higher education, government funded disability payments, General Assistance Unemployable (a program of cash, Food Stamps, and Medical insurance to people who are unable to work mostly due to conditions like depression) and a cornucopia of smaller bennies -- free bus passes and free cell phones.

The end result of all of this has been a total destruction of the mentality that prevailed in America before 1935 -- that of neighbor helping neighbor. During the Great Depression my grandfather brought home $300.00 per month and $100.00 was allocated to help out of work families in the neighborhood. My grandmother made certain that no child on the block went to school without a lunch. Fraternal organizations such as the Elks used to keep doctors on retainer for those who could not afford medical care. The loss of that mentality is a clear indicator of cultural decline; while Americans are still generous in giving money to charities, the *personal* involvement is gone. A quick look at the modern neighborhood will tell you that. Many of us don't even know the name of the person living next door. Why bother? If they are in any kind of need they can go to the Welfare office. Lots of help available there so I don't have to care.

2. *World War II (1941-1945)*

World War II had two major effects on our culture: **(1)** It ended the small town Norman Rockwell Americana and the traditional values that flourished in that environment. 15 million Americans -- mostly men -- entered the Armed Forces. This resulted in large scale family re-location and initiated the mobility and transiency that defines American society today, which can be summed up in one word -- *rootlessness*. People were uprooted from homes their families had lived in for generations either by the military or to take jobs in the defense industry located in large urban areas.

We completed the transition from an agrarian to an urban society during World War II and, as time passed, people-- and their values -- got lost in the anomie that defines urban life. In chapter 9 we will take a closer look at how this transition from an agrarian to an urban society became a crucial factor in the decline and fall of Traditional America; **(2)** World War II catapulted the United States into the position of World Leader. We emerged from the war as the world's only economic, industrial and military superpower. This gave us a prosperity that led to a new value system that placed emphasis on acquiring more money and material goods that were not available before the war. This had a negative impact on the family values that prevailed before the war.

The twenty years following World War II would sow the seeds for the collapse of the family and neighborhoods that defined the Old America.

3. *The "1950s" (1945-1965)*

The "1950s" were more of a cultural epoch than a chronological period. This era was both unique and a historical anomaly. We remember houses with unlocked doors, children playing outside unsupervised until after dark, dependable jobs, stable institutions, and people being overall prosperous, happy and optimistic about the future. We had a strong economy. We remember the iconic television images of the era -- *Ozzie and Harriet, Father Knows Best, Leave it to Beaver, The Donna Reed Show* -- that defined the period. Everyone knew their neighbors and we still had small mom and pop stores and restaurants in the neighborhood.

Yes, it was all of that. It was also a historical anomaly that could only exist as long as we were the world's sole industrial power. Russia was a super power at the time but that was primarily military. They had nowhere near the standard and quality of life that we enjoyed in the United States and their industrial capability was far below ours.

The 1950s was an artificial universe on a short timeline. It was a Potemkin Village society. In retrospect, the reason is obvious: **The 1950s era did not create and hand on its own moral capital; instead, we were living off the accumulated moral capital of pre-World War II America.**

On the outside we looked like a more prosperous version of the pre-war years; but we had stopped internalizing the values that had sustained earlier generations of Americans. Crime was low and church attendance was high but we were becoming addicted to our prosperity and we were planting the seeds of a narcissistic, materialist and consumerist culture. "Keeping up with the Joneses" became important. Married women started working outside the home to pay for second cars, vacation homes, and summer trips that were not there before World War II. Television replaced family conversation in the front room -- and on the front porch when the weather was nice. Parents wanted to give their children everything they did not have during the Depression, so Baby Boomers grew up getting too much handed to them and didn't have to earn their allowances as intensely as their parents had. This gave them a feeling and sense of *entitlement* that helped create present day America.

A "sub choke point" happened around 1957: stores started opening on Sunday; previously, retail stores were closed on Sundays. Restaurants and gas stations were opened but not department stores and many grocery stores. (Grocery stores that were open were governed by Blue Laws that restricted the sale of certain items on Sunday, especially alcoholic beverages.) he churches opposed this but the growing fixation with money and materialism won out. Today we have Black Friday (the day after Thanksgiving) with mobs queuing up in front of big box stores all night for a 5 A.M. (or earlier) opening that often results in fights over everything from TVs to waffle irons. One poor Walmart employee was trampled to death in 2008 as the mob stampeded in when he opened the doors.

A little noticed or discussed aspect of the 1950s was the beginning of the end of respect in the culture for men. Television sitcoms began portraying the bumbling husband and father. Two shows that underscored this were *The Life of Riley* and *The Honeymooners* -- and to a certain extent, *Ozzie and Harriet*. While most other sitcoms were not as emphatic on that point, most of them portrayed mom as being the real brains behind the household while the dads pursued their get-rich-quick schemes stumbling in and out of hilarious jams. If television is a mirror of the culture, then the family structure was beginning to crack ever so imperceptibly during the 1950s. This was linked to the New Materialism that was chipping away at all societal structures and institutions.

The 1950s ended in 1965 as Europe and Japan began to recover fully from World War II and would soon be giving us serious industrial competition. At the same time the, first wave of Baby Boomers began attending college, the Vietnam War was escalating, and the ink was barely dry on the 1964 Civil Rights Act. With Baby Boomers in college, an unpopular war expanding, and the cultural sea change in race relations, all fueled by an emerging drug culture, the 1950s were about to blow up -- literally. Here again is the reason for this cultural disintegration that was coming down on top of us:

The 1950s did not create and hand on its own moral capital; instead, we were living off the accumulated moral capital of pre-World War II America. By 1965 we had exhausted our stored up capital which the Boomers had never really internalized during their growing up years. Here comes 1966.

++

The following is a reflection by Gary Schouborg on why the 1950s ultimately failed and inevitably spawned the 1960s. The virtues and qualities Gary describes in the first half of this piece ushered in the 1950s but it was during the course of the 1950s that they began developing into what Gary discusses in the second half. From the vantage point of 2015 one can see how all of this developed slowly and was imperceptible to the people of the era.

Part of the problem is assuming that post-WW II was the normal state of affairs that somehow has gone awry. Little attention is paid to how that period was formed by an unusual convergence of factors.

1. Good times not taken for granted.

Society then was made up of people who had gone through the hardships of the Depression and WW II, which gave most people a sense that a comfortable living couldn't be taken for granted and had to be worked for.

2. We're in this together.

Bad times were sufficiently widespread in the Depression that people had a sense of sharing their situation. This group sense was furthered in the project of winning a major war that demanded that everyone participate.

3. Hard work rewarded.

The US alone escaped being devastated from the war, giving it a distinct but temporary competitive advantage. American workers could generally expect to be rewarded for their hard work.

4. Moral vision

The first three factors were aided and abetted by a commonly received morality that was seen as objective and that prioritized choices, resulting in relatively few goals, which could be shared.

(AUTHOR'S NOTE: The four characteristics Gary writes about were commonly held before and during World War II. They were still believed in by the adult generation during the 1950s but they became submerged in the materialism and consumerism that became overpowering distractors from those traditional American values; hence, they were not passed on in intact form to the Baby Boomers.)

This convergence began coming apart in the 60s.

1. Good times taken for granted.

The success of post-WW II 40s and 50s spawned a generation that saw the good times as their natural condition, weakening their motivation to work hard for what they wanted. **(AUTHOR'S NOTE: They were "entitled.")**

2. We're not in this together. (AUTHOR'S NOTE: It's all about _ME_.)

No one over 30 -- those who produced the good times now taken for granted --was to be trusted. The downside of the human rights movement Balkanized the country into hyphenated Americans with their distinctive interests.

3. Hard work not rewarded.

Reward for hard work was no longer guaranteed as international development began taking jobs even from those who were willing to work. **(AUTHOR'S NOTE: This continues to the present day as companies lay off employees at the drop of a hat showing no loyalty to their workers and then wonder why**

the employees are not loyal as they once were.)

4. No common moral vision

Philosophical progress exposed the (supposed) groundlessness of an abstract, objective, universal morality and has yet to replace it with a viable shared vision, leaving priorities up to each individual. People could therefore not agree on what good times were or to what degree they could be expected. Hard work was valued by some but not everyone. With the loss of a common moral vision came the loss of a sense of being in this together. Everyone doing their own thing inherently leads to Balkanization.

(AUTHOR'S NOTE: This supports our theorem that the cultural decline we are now experiencing took hold in the 1960s.)

(End of Gary Schouborg's reflection)

4. *The Birth Control Pill (1960)*

The oral contraceptive pill, next to tubal ligation and abstinence, is the surest way to prevent an unwanted pregnancy. In 1960 many doctors, for moral reasons refused to perform tubal ligations on women who had no children, especially if they were single. The pill took the fear and worry out of pre-marital and extra-marital sex. The fear of an unwanted pregnancy was a good deterrent to unmarried sex. The pill was a major driver of the Sexual Revolution of the later 1960s. Large families were common before the advent of the Birth Control Pill. Immediately after its introduction the number fell to the numbers we have today. The Pill explains the declining birth rate in Europe and North America.

Beyond this, The Pill had two serious side effects on the culture: **(1)** It diminished respect for the act of procreation and it is no coincidence that abortion became legal and acceptable within a few years after the advent of The Pill whereas before it had been illegal and stigmatized unless it was deemed medically necessary to save the mother's life; **(2)** Large families were conducive to the Common Good as children from large families had to learn to share and carry their share of the load in the family. They tended to be closer knit and more caring of one another's well-being. They learned to be better parents when their turn came. Children from much smaller families, and children with no siblings, were more self-centered and parents tended to cater to them and give them more stuff. This promoted a sense of entitlement. **(AUTHOR'S NOTE: I'm speaking from experience since I was an only child.)**

5. *The Abolition of School Prayer (1962)*

In 1962, The Supreme Supreme Court, in the Engle vs Vitale decision, banned school officials from composing a school prayer and encouraging its recitation in class.. This was followed in 1963 with the Abington School District vs Schempp decision, which banned school officials from organizing Bible reading or leading prayer in public schools. This has led to lower courts enacting a series of extremist interpretations of the Establishment Clause of the Constitution which states that the government "shall make no law respecting an establishment of religion or prohibiting the free exercise thereof."

(AUTHOR'S NOTE: These decisions were aimed at school officials and teachers but did not directly ban students from praying or studying the Bible or performing other religious activities on their own at school as long as there was no school sponsorship; however, Political Correctness and Multiculturalism have done that. Political Correctness and Multiculturalism have the force of law today.)

Since then, the government has increasingly suppressed religious activities on public property -- Manger scenes at Christmas in government buildings and public schools, prayers before sporting events, student Bible clubs on school grounds, and memorial crosses on public lands, among others. The word "Christmas" has been banned in some school districts in favor of "winter" as in "winter concert" in place of Christmas concert (Appropriate in that "winter" is a cold replacement for the spiritual warmth of the Christmas season.)

The Establishment Clause was set up to prevent the establishment of a State sponsored Church as was the case in so many European countries in the 18th century. These State controlled Churches often persecuted or discriminated against other religions. The Founders did not want that repeated here since so many had come to America to escape religious persecution in search of religious freedom.

School Prayer had nothing to do with a State run Church or the "establishment of religion."

And while there is no empirical evidence, there is plenty of anecdotal evidence to suggest that the collapse of the American Public Education system began shortly after the school prayer ban went into effect. There were no school shootings and very few violent assaults on teachers and other students. There is no way to prove a connection but it is interesting to note how quickly both academics and safety deteriorated in public schools after 1962; just something to think about.

This is a major choke point since it was the beginning of the removal of God from every aspect of public life-- another example of a "slippery slope." The Supreme Court totally ignored the second part of the Establishment Clause about prohibiting the free exercise of religion.

6. *The Immigration Reform Act of 1965*

(AUTHOR'S NOTE: The following quotation is from the Wikipedia article on the Immigration Reform Act.)

The 1965 act marked a radical break from the immigration policies of the past. The law as it stood then excluded Asians and Africans and preferred northern and western Europeans over southern and eastern ones. At the height of the civil rights movement of the 1960s the law was seen as an embarrassment by, among others, President John F. Kennedy, who called the then-quota-system 'nearly intolerable.' After Kennedy's assassination, President Lyndon Johnson signed the bill at the foot of the Statue of Liberty as a symbolic gesture.

In order to convince the American populace - the majority of who were opposed to the act - of the legislation's merits, its liberal proponents assured that passage would not influence America's culture significantly. President Johnson called the bill "not revolutionary", Secretary of State Dean Rusk estimated only a few thousand Indian immigrants over the next five years, and other politicians, including Senator Ted Kennedy, hastened to reassure the populace that the demographic mix would not be affected; these assertions would later prove wildly inaccurate. In line with earlier immigration law, the bill also prohibited the entry into the country of 'sexual deviants', including homosexuals. By doing so it crystallized the policy of the INS that had previously been rejecting homosexual immigrants on the grounds that they were 'mentally defective' or had a 'constitutional psychopathic inferiority.

(End of Wikipedia article)

This act, plus a porous southern border explains why we have an estimated 13 million illegal aliens in the United States today. Employers saw a cheap source of labor and Democratic politicians saw votes. Illegals are eligible for driver's licenses in some states and their children are authorized to receive free public education. 15 States allow in-state college tuition discounts to illegals. Potential for election fraud increases markedly in states that do not require photo ID to vote. Illegal immigration is costing Federal, state and local governments billions of dollars and more are coming across the southern border every day. Since the U.S. government does not enforce immigration laws, illegals know they can stay.

According to the Center for Immigration Studies, there are more than 200 American cities that have declared themselves "Sanctuary Cities" refusing to comply with Federal Immigration laws by offering safe haven to illegal immigrants. The Federal Government under President Barack Obama supports the concept of Sanctuary Cities. As of this writing, the Sanctuary City movement is under fire due to a murder committed by an illegal immigrant in San Francisco who, after multiple felonies and deportations, headed for San Francisco because of its lenient Sanctuary City policies. The official justification for Sanctuary Cities, never mind that they are in direct violation of Federal Law, is that they will take the fear out of illegals reporting crimes to the police. This is bogus since illegals reporting crimes are eligible for U Visas from the State Department which will protect them from deportation; in reality, Sanctuary Cities offer safe havens and hideouts to criminal illegals as the tragedy in San Francisco shows. Sanctuary Cities are examples of the emotion based false compassion for illegals driven by a guilt that we will discuss further in the root causes of Multiculturalism.

In December 2014, President Obama "temporarily" legalized five million illegals by Executive order. This will only encourage further illegal immigration.

Legal immigrants can bring in family members placing a burden on social services. Government agencies are required to accommodate immigrants by providing services in their own language or providing interpreters. Immigrants feel less need to assimilate and are forming political interest and action groups based on nationality. Different immigrant groups are involved in organized crime -- Mexican and Central American drug gangs and Russian mafias are the best organized.

Many immigrants coming over legally make the Welfare Office their first stop. Depending on the state, they care eligible to receive a generous package of benefits including cash, Food Stamps, Medicaid, housing, and education. In the Ukraine there are classes teaching potential immigrants how to use the Welfare system in this country. Illegal immigrants are not legally entitled to Welfare but there are plenty of ways to circumvent the system through family members who are legal residents and, of course, outright fraud.

This is not an indictment of all immigrants. Many come over here to live the American Dream, or what was once the American Dream. But too many are abusing the system and the unholy alliance of businesses looking for cheap labor, politicians looking for votes, and a Secular Progressive Establishment that screams racism and xenophobia whenever anyone tries to seriously address the problem, has had a polarizing effect on the American cultural landscape. What we have now is a formula for Balkanization and the marginalization of traditional American culture that made it possible and attractive for immigrants to come here in the first place. Nothing has a more devastating effect on a Prevalent Culture than government enforced Multiculturalism which we will discuss in further.

The original immigrant goal was assimilation and Americanization. Today, with a political establishment that panders to immigrants, they see no need to assimilate. In heavy Latino areas, the public schools often submerge the Traditional culture in favor of the Hispanic culture. We will discuss some examples of this.

7. *The '60s Era (1966-1973)*

Like the 1950s, this was a cultural epoch instead of a chronologically defined decade.   This period witnessed the most profound and rapid cultural change in history. The era was divided into four components.

The Vietnam War

This conflict enjoyed popular support until 1966 when it became clear that we were getting bogged down and had no clear objective. The stated purpose was to keep Southeast Asia (South Vietnam, Cambodia, Laos, Thailand, and Malaysia) from falling under Communist (Russian or Chinese) control. Draft calls approached 50,000 per month during the summer of 1966. This caused anti-war demonstrations among college students who were of draft age.

The war became increasingly unpopular as we poured billions of dollars and hundreds of thousands of soldiers into what was rapidly becoming a no-win war. The government would not do what was necessary to win and end the war -- invade North Vietnam; instead, they contained it to "search and destroy" operations in the south and bombing raids over North Vietnam while the Johnson Administration micromanaged the war from the White House making it even more difficult for the military to accomplish any worthwhile objectives. This period saw the beginning of the American Left's home grown anti-Americanism that painted the United States as an aggressor and oppressive nation, a perception that has become institutionalized today.

We would pull out of South Vietnam in 1973 and the country would fall to the North Vietnamese Communists in April 1975. Cambodia and Laos came under the control of their indigenous Communist insurgency groups, the Khmer Rouge and Pathet Lao at the same time; all this after losing more than 58,000 soldiers and probably a trillion dollars.

This marked the beginning of a downward trend in our military and foreign policy (except for a brief resurgence during the Reagan Presidency, 1981-89) that would persist into the 21st century as we continue to fight the war on Islamic Jihadists. We are employing the same "search and destroy" aimlessness as public opinion rapidly turns against government policy and the Administration looks for exit strategies instead of winning strategies. We duplicated Vietnam in Iraq and now that country is unraveling after our departure. Afghanistan is the next country where we are employing the "Vietnam paradigm" both in the way we fight it and the way we leave it.

We cannot exit a war before it is won, relying on the local army to take over the management of the war no matter how much we train them. This is what happened in Vietnam and Iraq, and is following the same course in Afghanistan.

(AUTHOR'S NOTE: We left no residual force in either Vietnam or Iraq. The Communist North Vietnamese conquered South Vietnam and ISIS Jihadists are now in the process of conquering Iraq. The Obama Administration now says it will leave a residual force in Afghanistan but for how long? When these troops withdraw, Afghanistan falls.)

Vietnam has come to define our military policy and, to a large extent, our foreign policy.to the present day. The only exception was the Reagan Administration which employed an effective strategy that brought down the Soviet Union and gained freedom for Eastern Europe. He used economic warfare and while it did increase considerably our National Debt, it put an end to a power that had been a threat to world stability since the end of World War II without costing the life of one American soldier.

The Civil Rights Movement

The Civil Rights Movement first came into the national spotlight in the 1950s when the Federal Government began forcibly desegregating public schools in the South in enforcement of the 1954 United States Supreme Court decision, Brown vs Board of Education of Topeka, that declared school segregation by race to be unconstitutional. In 1957, President Eisenhower sent in Federal troops to desegregate Central High School in Little Rock, Arkansas and in 1962 President Kennedy sent in the troops to desegregate the University of Mississippi. In 1964 President Johnson signed the Civil Rights Act into Law barring all discrimination based on race, gender, or religion.

Riots soon followed -- Watts (Los Angeles) in 1965, Detroit, Newark and other cities over the next three years. Demonstrating and rioting were made fashionable due to the passions fueled by the anti-Vietnam War movement and the empowerment of Blacks by the recently signed Civil Rights Act. Support from the Intellectual Elite -- the universities, the media, and the entertainment industry -- gave these movements further impetus. The anti-war and Civil Rights movements enshrined these three institutions as molders of public opinion.

The Civil Rights movement accomplished a great deal toward ending discrimination but it came with an unintended consequence -- dislike for Whites among many Blacks as Black leaders -- Jesse Jackson, Louis Farrakhan, Al Sharpton and others kept telling Blacks that they were victims and that they had to keep on fighting for their rights. After initial beneficial successes and accomplishments, the Civil Rights Movement became a polarizing force in American society.

(AUTHOR'S NOTE: Throughout this book I come across as being harsh in my assessment of the Black Community. This may seem unfair since the majority of Black Americans are fine people. But there are serious issues in the Black community that are destroying it; and, while there are many good mentoring groups in the Black Community working with at risk youth, the entire community must get on board since these groups lack the resources to reach all those needing help. The root of all these issues is the disintegration of the Black family, once the strongest in the country. Without a restoration of the Black family, the Black community will be irretrievably lost. Yet a vocal and influential group within the Black community refuses to acknowledge and address the loss of the Black family while blaming "White Privilege", the police and White culture in general. We will return to this issue throughout the book.)

The Civil Rights Act was a two-sided coin. On one side, something had to be done about the situation in the South. It was blatantly wrong and nothing short of institutionalized racism when American citizens had to ride in the back of the bus or give up their seat to a White person, to use separate drinking fountains, use different restrooms, or eat in the restaurant kitchen. Some amusement parks and theaters had separate days or Blacks. This is a permanent blemish on American history. Government action was necessary but when any kind of cultural evolution-- good or bad -- is forced, there is going to be violence and backlash. There was plenty of violence in the 1960s and continuing backlash is the tenuous state of race relations in America today.

Today the focus is on relations between the Black community and the police since: as of this writing, the past year has seen riots in Ferguson, Missouri, New York City, and Baltimore, Maryland where Blacks have died during confrontations with police officers. This has led to rioting and subsequent looting and property destruction reminiscent of the late 1960s. The demonstrations are fueled by emotion and escalate out of control before all the facts are in.

Another unintended consequence of the Civil Rights Movement was the disintegration of the Black family. Welfare and the Sexual Revolution were factors in this disintegration but there may be other factors in play here; The Blacks in the South went from oppressive segregation, often backed up with banana republic police brutality, to full legal equality in just two s years -- 1964 to 1966. Soon after that they were given preference in hiring thanks to Affirmative Action.

While conditions were better for Blacks in the North -- no segregation or "Jim Crow" laws enforcing it -- they were still treated like second class citizens. They could not join a wide variety of different social organizations and could not live in many neighborhoods. They were not legally banned from living in these neighborhoods -- people simply would not sell to them and there were no laws in place against doing that; so things changed quickly for northern Blacks as well.

There are two other factors we need to consider: **(1)** It is possible that changes came too quickly for the Black community in America to absorb and adapt? These changes were absolutely necessary and needed to come quickly from the aspect of justice but the human psyche needs time to adapt. A similar scenario unfolded with the collapse of the Soviet Union and the Russian attempt to implement a Free Market economy overnight. After 75 years of Communist dictatorship, the people were not able to psychologically process the freedom that had come upon them so quickly. Chaos ensued, followed by economic anarchy and the rise of the Russian Mafia. For change to be effective, it needs to come incrementally; if not, it takes a toll on the human psyche since the human mind has difficulty processing sudden and rapid change; **(2)** There was no leadership in the Black Community to guide them through this process. If Martin Luther King had survived would things have been different? (Could he have been the first Black president? He would have been 63 in 1992.) There were no Black leaders of any regional or national stature to address out-of-wedlock birth rates and crime rates before they got out of control. The so-called Black "leaders" mentioned above were demagogues that kept drilling into the Black community the idea that they are victims, that racism is still pandemic and Blacks cannot get fair treatment in White America. It is to their advantage to keep the Black community down. They are the equivalents ofDathan the overseer in *The Ten Commandments* who profited and advanced his position through the misery of his people. These "leaders" have convinced many Blacks through implication that it is hopeless since White dominated society is determined to keep them down. This has particularly affected many young Black males who have lost all incentive to try, leading them to become involved in crime (usually drugs). Today approximately 25 percent of Black males between the ages of 18 and 29 are in jail, on probation or on parole. This is why there is so much tension between the police and the Black Community.

Many Black men abandon their children and each succeeding generation feels this is the norm. Whites no longer shun Blacks because of their race but because they are frustrated by the chaos in the Black community. It's a different racial dynamic than it was in the pre-Civil Rights era. White Americans take a similar attitude towards Latinos because of the illegal immigration problem, the gang problem and the high out-of-wedlock birth rate. It is no longer racial bias; it is racial frustration on the part of the White community. Secular Progressive politicians use these differences as a "divide and conquer" wedge to get votes. It has led to Balkanization and mutual distrust among the races. Strong positive leadership in minority communities could go a long way in solving these issues but it isn't there. The "leadership" that is there continues to stoke the fire and stir the pot for their own gain.

Change has to come from within these communities since Whites are labeled as racist and anti-immigrant when they try to weigh in. The Black and Hispanic communities have a solid religious foundation and their churches should be providing leadership but all American churches are failing in Leadership.

A racially divided country will never be a strong country and race relations only seem to be getting worse.

The Sexual Revolution

The anti-war and Civil Rights demonstrations brought large groups of young people together who were rebelling, not only against the war and racial discrimination, but also against the older generation whom they believed were perpetuating and supporting these events (the war and racial discrimination). This led to a rejection of all the values held by their parents' generation, especially sexual "repression." Their attitude was "if it feels good, do it." The fairly recent (at the time) addition of the Birth Control Pill to pharmacology facilitated the process. Easy sex led to a breakdown of traditional morality. "Why buy the whole cow when the milk's so cheap" -- in other words, why get married when we can just live together without any commitment? Is it any wonder that the out-of-wedlock birth skyrocketed in the wake of the Sexual Revolution? (Not everyone remembered to take preventive measures in the heat of passion -- and making babies increased Welfare benefits.)

Easy sex diminished marriage since the social stigma of pre-marital sex and having babies out of wedlock was no longer there. Divorce rates climbed. Television and movies, the mirror of the culture, celebrated extramarital sex. Casual sex soon became a staple of TV sitcoms that at one time prohibited TV couples from sharing the same bed if they were not actually married to one another. Parents became more accepting of this new behavior since they did not want to "alienate" their children. As recently as the early 1960s, children ran the risk of being disowned by their parents for pre-marital sex (as one grade school friend of mine was); by the end of the 1960s, they and their live-in partners were sharing quarters with mom and dad.

Same sex relationships that were still out of the mainstream during the 1960s Sexual Revolution are now acceptable without question and same sex marriage is legal throughout the country by fiat of the U.S. Supreme Court. There is already a show on cable TV called *Sister Wives* about a polygamous marriage. (It appears that we are still sliding down that slippery slope.) Another side effect of the Sexual Revolution seems to be a growing disenchantment with the institution of marriage. 2013 (the last year that statistics are currently available) recorded the lowest number of marriages in the United States since they started keeping records.

Ask yourself how many people you know, especially younger people, who are living together and/or have out-of-wedlock children either with each other or other partners. Your own circle of friends, acquaintances, co-workers and associates should provide some interesting statistics.

The Drug Scene

Drugs have always been around but widespread usage began in the mid-1960s. Young people were experimenting with civil disobedience; sex and rebelling against their parents so drugs were a natural. "If my parents can smoke cigarettes then I can smoke marijuana -- and cocaine -- and drop acid (LSD)." This trend was fueled by Hard Rock and Heavy Metal music, more cultural by-products of the late 1960s that glorified drug use featuring band members who openly used rugs. And it wasn't only band members and entertainment celebrities, it was also Harvard professor Timothy Leary who advocated the use of LSD and encouraged young people to "turn on, tune in, and drop out." Drugs became just another tool of rebellion by a rebellious generation. Drugs were illegal and looked down on by the "Establishment"; therefore, they must be good and they made you feel good too. This generated the expression "if you remember the 60s you weren't there" since you had to be stoned to "be there" and if you were stoned all the time you wouldn't remember any of it.

The Hippie movement was the product and direct result of all four of these components. Their way of life was sex, drugs, and heavy metal music. They often lived in "communes" -- old houses and farms. Most of the communes didn't last long because the occupants were too stoned or too busy having sex (euphemistically known as "free love") to do any work to maintain the commune and keep it going. The "Manson Family," a Hippie commune under the leadership of "cult guru" Charles Manson, were heavy drug users and devotees of group sex. Their version of the "Summer of Love" ended in August 1969 when they committed the Tate-LaBianca murders. (See chapter 4) This put the whole Hippie movement in a bad light and it faded away over the next couple of years. The Manson gang signaled the beginning of the end of the Hippie movement.

Someone once said of the '60s: "It was a great party but the hangover is still with us." Today all the sexual taboos, except rape, incest and pedophilia, are gone, half the marriages end in divorce, out-of-wedlock births are common since we don't stigmatize that anymore by stamping the birth certificate with the word "illegitimate" as that is a demeaning term. Yes, it is but how many out-of-wedlock births did that concept prevent?

Drug usage is rampant and drug selling gangs (both domestic and foreign) are in every major city. The American addiction to drugs is keeping at least six Mexican drug cartels in business and this is posing a serious threat to our southern border and overall national security.

Now there is a trend to legalize small amounts of marijuana. Both Washington State and Colorado passed measures legalizing marijuana in the November 2012 elections. Many, even in the conservative camp, feel that the cost of enforcement and interdiction is no longer worth it and we should legalize all drugs and tax them, never mind the physical and mental damage they inflict. Most people recognize the medical and psychological damage from hard drugs and there are conflicting studies and reports about marijuana but ingesting carbon monoxide and incinerated vegetation cannot be good for anyone's health; furthermore, the intent of marijuana usage is to get an immediate high unlike cigarettes (which are no good either). Getting stoned is just another version of getting drunk but you can have a couple of beers and a couple glasses of wine or a couple of highballs without getting drunk. Marijuana beams you straight up to Scotty. Today's marijuana is much more potent than it was in the 1960s. Widespread drug use undermines the fabric of society. You can't have a healthy and productive society if a significant percentage of the population is stoned at any given time.

It is phenomenal how quickly these changes overwhelmed American society and changed it for the worse. When I graduated from high school in 1964 beer on Friday night and teen-age cigarette smoking was as bad as it got. By 1966 marijuana and hard drugs were all over the place including the high schools.

Teen-age sex was happening when I was in school (and those who were doing it kept quiet) but not on the large scale it was occurring two years later. I remember a conversation between myself and two friends when I was a junior in high school -- we were trying to figure out who might be having sex at our school. Today it would be who isn't having sex? In 1964 most of us hadn't ever heard of Vietnam and couldn't find it on a map. Two years later we were worried about getting drafted and sent there

The 1960s were more than a cultural choke point -- they were a mini cultural epoch. We will look at cultural epochs in chapter 13.

8. *Affirmative Action (1960s-Present)*

We have included this cultural choke point in the 1970s since that is when its impact became noticeable in the culture.

The following article is from Wikipedia.

The concept of affirmative action was introduced in the early 1960s in the United States, as a way to combat racial discrimination in the hiring process and, in 1967, the concept was expanded to include sex. Affirmative action was first created from Executive Order 10925, which was signed by President John F. Kennedy on 6 March 1961 and required that government employers "not discriminate against any employee or applicant for employment because of race, creed, color, or national origin" and "take affirmative action to ensure that applicants are employed, and that employees are treated during employment, without regard to their race, creed, color, or national origin."

On 24 September 1965, President Lyndon B. Johnson signed Executive Order 11246, thereby replacing Executive Order 10925 and affirming Federal Government's commitment "to promote the full realization of equal employment opportunity through a positive, continuing program in each executive department and agency".[Affirmative action was extended to women by Executive Order 11375 which amended Executive Order 11246 on 13 October 1967, by adding "sex" to the list of protected categories. In the U.S. affirmative action's original purpose was to pressure institutions into compliance with the nondiscrimination mandate of the Civil Rights Act of 1964. The Civil Rights Acts do not cover veterans, people with disabilities, or people over 40. These groups are protected from discrimination under different laws.

Affirmative action has been the subject of numerous court cases, and has been questioned upon its constitutional legitimacy. In 2003, a Supreme Court decision regarding affirmative action in higher education (*Grutter v. Bollinger*, 539 US 244 – Supreme Court 2003) permitted educational institutions to consider race as a factor when admitting students. Alternatively, some colleges use financial criteria to attract racial groups that have typically been under-represented and typically have lower living conditions. Some states such as California (California Civil Rights Initiative), Michigan (Michigan Civil Rights Initiative), and Washington (Initiative 200) have passed constitutional amendments banning public institutions, including public schools, from practicing affirmative action within their respective states. Conservative activists have alleged that colleges quietly use illegal quotas to increase the number of minorities and have launched numerous lawsuits to stop them.

(End of Wikipedia article)

Affirmative Action is a direct refutation of Martin Luther King's "I Have a Dream" speech where he said that people should be judged "by the content of their character and not the color of their skin." (or gender)

9. *Women's Liberation (1970s)*

Like most "Rights" movements, Women's Liberation addressed some legitimate grievances. Women often did not receive the same pay in the private sector as men performing the same jobs. They were virtually barred from top level corporate jobs and were kept out of certain occupations considered "men only" -- construction, longshoring and long haul truck driving along with some of the trades -- electrician and plumber. A woman often had to have a male co-signer to open a credit or checking account. (That was probably a carryover from the days when few women had paid employment and, if they did, it was likely to be low paying.)

All of this was clearly wrong. And, like most "Rights" movements, Women's Liberation pushed the envelope far beyond simple equality. They, like minorities, got on the Affirmative Action band wagon demanding and receiving preferential consideration in hiring and promotions; and like most "Rights" movements; this one found an enemy -- White males. Women's Liberation bred the Feminist Movement, a charter member of The Society of the Perpetually Offended. Men had to walk on egg shells to avoid offending women or they might find themselves slapped with sexual harassment charges which always carried a guilty verdict. Complementing a woman on her appearance could be considered sexual harassment and employers, ever fearful of lawsuits, caved in and met their demands.

For a while, during the 1970s, Feminist propaganda was trying to sell society on the idea that fathers were unnecessary and, given the large number of single mothers, they had some degree of success. Gloria Steinhem told women that they needed a man "like a fish needs a bicycle." Colleges and universities that were formerly men only had to enroll women. But women's colleges were not under the same pressure. Today there are sixty women's colleges in the United States and only four all male colleges. All male clubs such as The Elks had to admit women. A glance at Wikipedia reveals approximately fifty all women's organizations. There is no pressure on women's organizations to admit men. Promise Keepers, an all-male Christian group dedicating themselves to becoming better husbands and fathers, was attacked by Feminists as being sexist and patriarchal supporting male dominance. We never hear that about the National Organization of Women doing that for women. All male clubs and organizations are regarded as discriminatory, sexist and misogynist and face government penalties if they refuse to admit women. Women's organizations face no such pressure.

(AUTHOR'S NOTE: I researched the internet for the number of all men's organizations still functioning in this country. Not only could I find no information but I encountered an article stating that the writer couldn't find any information on that topic either. Interesting!)

While much of the early "all men are rapists" fanaticism has subsided, men in 2015 have been subtly relegated to the status of second class citizens. Female virtues and characteristics are praised as being good for society while male behavior is "violent" and "abusive." Today's culture discourages boys from playing with toy guns because it encourages violenc**e. (AUTHOR'S NOTE: It didn't have that effect when I was growing up in the 1950s when there was much less violent crime and no school shootings.)**

Where a man is "aggressive" or "belligerent", a woman is merely being "assertive." Women's issues receive far more coverage than men's. Bookstores have numerous books for women but for men it's usually restricted to the anger management genre. There are many more social programs aimed at helping women than at helping men. How many marches do you see for prostate cancer compared to those for breast cancer? An estimated 65 percent of the male population will develop prostate cancer at some time in their lives.

Women's Liberation has created tensions between men and women that never used to exist in our culture. At one time we respected the differences between men and women and good natured humor was common between the genders. When my mother owned her café in the 1950s one of the male customers always used to greet her by saying "Hi, Blondie." Today that would be unacceptable. A man dare not call a female co-worker "honey," "sweetie", or "love" without fear of repercussions including getting sued or fired. But women can pretty much say or do that they want with no problem. Men actually like it (and I think a lot of women would enjoy it too). I once got a good natured slap on the fanny from a female co-worker. I thought it was cute. Could a man do that to a female co-worker? Yeah, right!

Women's Liberation has destroyed mutual respect between the genders. An unintended consequence of this has been the dramatic rise in domestic violence. Fifty years ago there were strong social taboos against hitting a woman. It happened then but not in the volume it occurs today. Part of the reason for this is that when Women's Liberation decreed fathers to be unnecessary, a lot of men deserted the household leaving no solid male role model to teach boys how to act like real men (gentlemen) around women.

There IS a purpose as to why the two genders function differently -- they are "hardwired" to do so. You cannot eliminate those differences by legislative fiat reinforced by Political Correctness, and expect to have a healthy culture. The result is frustration, mistrust and hostility.

It was part of the natural cultural evolution of society that women would start coming into the work place in large numbers but it has not been a totally positive development for the culture. Women began evolving into the career track with the Baby Boom generation as an increasing number of women began going to college. The combination of the new found post-war prosperity, expanding career and job opportunities and technological advances propelled more young men and women than ever before into college and graduate school after that. (Today women outnumber men in college.)

The post-World War II era was the first time in history that jobs and careers were more available to women. Before the war most jobs were "heavy lifting" that most women were not physically capable of doing. With the rapid increases in technology, more career opportunities opened up for them. But the family unit suffered. The family is always strongest and the Common Good best served when the man earns the living and the woman runs the household and is there for the children. That may not be fashionable -- or even fair by today's standards -- but it worked. Some families have stay-at-home dads where the mom is the breadwinner but even in today's "liberated" culture the stay-at-home "nanny dad" is quietly viewed as a loser.

All women need marketable skills today since they cannot rely on a man (husband) to take care of them. The blurred roles of men and women, the lack of traditional male role models and the overall downplaying of the male role in today's society have made men less dependable and responsible -- the self-fulfilling prophecy.

Today an increasing number of women feel like they were sold a "bill of goods" with that Feminist propaganda about "having it all"-- a family and a career. Women with younger children wish they could stay home (especially single mothers balancing family, work and daycare arrangements) but the cost of living has adjusted to "dual careers" and two incomes are now essential in most households. Like most men, most women have jobs rather than "careers" and the romance of "having it all" is fading into mythology.

Men have been major casualties of the Women's movement. In order to accomplish their goals, Feminists demonized men to the extent that they are becoming embedded into the cultural psyche as abusers, pedophiles, deadbeat dads and losers until proven otherwise. A man dare not talk to a child he doesn't know; a woman can but a man can't. Political Correctness that protects so many different groups in today's society allows for all sorts of verbal abuse directed at men, especially White men. I recently heard a caller on the *Michael Medved* radio talk show, a White male himself, define White males over 50 as "racists and bigots." This is a widely held opinion in contemporary culture. White females are not labeled thusly. Minority males are protected from this sort of demonization by their race. The Feminist movement has been a polarizing factor in our culture.

For further reading I recommend *Men on Strike* by Helen Smith Ph.D that goes in depth about the current alienation of men in contemporary society. Her premise is that men are giving up in our society by not going to college, not getting married and not establishing careers in the numbers they did before the enshrinement of Feminism in our culture. *The War on Boys* by Christina Hoff Sommers details the campaign in the culture to make boys more like girls. This may be happening since the Millennial males of today seem to be different from young males of previous generations. This is a purely anecdotal observation but those of us from the Baby Boomer generation had a different bearing when we were that age. (We will discuss this phenomenon further in chapter 11.) There are marked differences in cultural outlook between the generations. Christina Hoff Sommers shows a societal pattern of "feminizing" boys that has been going on for at least the past couple of decades. There is no doubt that in gender relations, as in race relations, we have become a polarized culture and cultural growth and development becomes impossible in this kind of environment.

Feminists seem to forget that they could have never made the gains they did without the active co-operation of men. Men were proactive in advancing women's rights in the workplace. And here's another interesting point to ponder: Women never felt "oppressed" until they were told they were victims of a patriarchal society by their self-appointed advocates. Roles were clearly defined: men dealt with the outside world and women ran the house and it worked. Both genders had their spheres of control and influence.

(10. *Legalization of Abortion (1973)*

Prior to the Roe v Wade Supreme Court decision that legalized abortion on demand in 1973 (some states had had legalized it a few years before that.), it was only legal when the life of the mother was in clear jeopardy. Today we have late term abortions that kill viable babies. I wouldn't call them fetuses at eight and a half months but they can be legally taken from the womb at that point and killed. (Babies can survive outside the womb at 20 weeks.) There have been approximately 55 million legal abortions in the United States since Roe v Wade in 1973. If there ever was an argument for the "slippery slope" theory, it is abortion.

The birth control pill created license for worry free extra-marital sex and, as this increased, so did the number of unintended pregnancies. ("I forgot to take the pill" was a frequent excuse.) This is why Planned Parenthood was a strong supporter of artificial contraception; it would prevent unwanted pregnancies. But it didn't in too many instances so Planned Parenthood became the leading advocate for abortion on demand in the United States.

The now easy acceptance of abortion has seeped into the cultural psyche and diminished respect for human life at all levels. The good news is that there is growing opposition for abortion for just any reason and for late term abortions in particular, but the majority of the public favors it in cases of rape or incest and tolerates first trimester abortions. Yet, as evil as rape and incest are, the fetus is still a human life. If we delve deeply enough into our own ancestry it is almost inevitable that we are all descendants of a rape case. The number of our ancestors doubles with every generation. Going back 10 generations we have over 1000 progenitors and that keeps doubling with every generation so it's all but inevitable there is a rape back there somewhere that, if it hadn't happened, we would not be here. That in NO WAY justifies the crime and sin of rape but facts are facts nonetheless. It just proves that God brings good out of evil actions.

The Republican Party Platform is on record as opposing abortion on demand but has been unsuccessful in overturning Roe v. Wade since abortion is a cultural rather than a political issue and the culture needs to change before abortion can be done away with. That is the nature of democracy. There is little chance of that since the Secular Progressive tsunami is sweeping the culture further and further away from the traditional moral foundations (Judeo-Christian) upon which the United States was founded.

Abortion arguably gives us moral equivalency with Nazi Germany, especially in light of a story in the news at the present time. A pro-life group, The Center for Medical Progress, has conducted undercover video stings of interviews with Planned Parenthood doctors about the sale of body parts from aborted fetuses which is against the law. Some of the doctors interviewed were laughing about it -- one referred to "crunchy" body parts. The whole atmosphere was callous disregard. Perhaps moral equivalency with Nazi Germany is a harsh indictment but they killed millions of people they could see. We are slaughtering millions of people we cannot see, so what's the difference? Planned Parenthood's disposition of body parts is straight out of the Mengele playbook. Abortion and its consequences have turned us into a barbaric nation. Nazi Germany and Stalin's Russia were barbaric nations. So, I ask again -- what's the difference? We have become as morally bankrupt as those evil regimes.

11. *Watergate (1972-74)*

On June 17, 1972 some Nixon staffers broke into the headquarters of the Democratic National Committee at their suite of offices in the Watergate office complex (hence the name of the scandal) in Washington, D.C. The Nixon Administration tried to cover it up but the scandal exploded in the press leading to Nixon's resignation in August 1974. A number of his staffers were sentenced to Federal prison terms for their part in the break in and cover up.

The national news media made a big deal out of this relatively low level beef because they hated Richard Nixon who didn't help matters any by covering up and lying about it.

There are three reasons why Watergate is a cultural choke point: **(1)** Watergate institutionalized the national news media's unswerving loyalty and dedication to the Democratic Party and their Secular Progressive agenda that had taken full hold during the presidential campaign of George

McGovern in 1972. After Watergate, nearly all of the media tilted Democrat; **(2)** The beginning of the polarizing partisanship that has today paralyzed government to the point where it is practically impossible to enact legislation unless one Party controls the White House, Senate, and House of Representatives. This began with the 75 freshmen Democratic representatives elected in 1974 in the wake of Watergate who block voted Democrat on every issue. It has only gotten worse. Today there is thinly veiled hatred between the two Parties. While both Parties have always had fundamental philosophical differences, the Party out of power used to be known as "the loyal opposition." The operative word was "loyal." That concept is now extinct; **(3)** Watergate generated a deep mistrust and cynicism toward government on the part of the American people. Previously, Americans had a naïve trust in government. I mentioned earlier my aunt saying: "If you can't trust the government, who can you trust?" Part of this was due to the fact that the press most of the time withheld any hint of political misbehavior from the public. President Kennedy's now notorious philandering was unknown to the general public during his presidency. Scandals did leak through occasionally but, by and large, the American public naively trusted government prompting H.L. Mencken to label Americans as "The Boobsoisie." His best known quotation to this effect was from his July 26, 1920 column in the Baltimore Sun Times:

"As democracy is perfected, the office of President represents, more and more closely, the inner soul of the people. On some great and glorious day the plain folks of the land will reach their heart's desire at last and the White House will be occupied by a downright fool and complete narcissistic moron."

12. *The Decline of the Entertainment Industry and the Loss of a Classic Literary Tradition. (1960s to present)*

The entertainment industry (movies, television and music) has been pandering to the lowest common denominator of public taste since the late 1960s. The majority of movies (there are some exceptions) are a tour de force of gratuitous sex and violence or exercises in stupidity. The entertainment industry makes fun of traditional values and portrays those who subscribe to them as unenlightened rubes. *Dogma, Jesus Camp, Monty Python's Meaning of Life. The Magdalene Sisters, The Boys of St. Vincent,* and *The name of the Rose* are just a few examples of movies that trash Christianity or make it look stupid and repressive. There are many more -- some subtle, some blatant. Television is a showcase of vacuous twenty-somethings who cannot think of or talk about anything except sex. *Two and a half Men* is a good example of this genre although the two protagonists are around 40.

Television, being the mirror of a society that is becoming increasingly dysfunctional is featuring more "reality" shows about dysfunctional people and dysfunctional families. *The Osbornes* were one of the first of this type. Other shows featured a group of women competing to marry a self-proclaimed millionaire whom they had never met. The marriage, shown on national television, not surprisingly ended in a speedy divorce; overweight people displaying their struggles to "get down" to 600 pounds so a doctor can perform surgery on them to facilitate further weight loss; hoarders resisting all attempts of others to persuade them to rid themselves of their floor-to-ceiling, wall-to-wall junk and (sometimes literal) crap collections; drama princesses in terminal angst over $25000.00 wedding dresses; various "survival" type shows with one called *Naked and Afraid* that introduces a man and a woman, usually in the Millennial age group, who meet for the first time after stripping naked in preparation for spending 21 days together surviving in jungles and on deserted islands. *Sister Wives* recounts the adventures of polygamist Kody Brown, his four wives and their 17 children.

The longest running of these horror shows is *The Jerry Springer Show* which runs five days a week. It has three segments per show with young couples airing their dirty laundry on nationwide television. The standard format is Larry Loser confessing to his girlfriend (or spouse) that he is cheating. The woman he is cheating with comes out on stage and the two females break into a rolling on the floor hair pulling match to the tune of a ringside bell; or Tina Trailertrash confesses to Billy Bob that she is cheating on him, often with his soon-to-be ex best friend. The other guy comes out and a fist fight ensues occasionally with the two men taking off their shirts and fighting bare chested. Nearly every segment has a fight scene. This show has to be an act; if it isn't that means there are an overwhelming number of dysfunctional nut cases walking around at large in this country. Most of the males appearing on this show don't have a job or just got out of jail. The shows feature Gay and Lesbian couples and threesomes as well. *Springer* has at least two clones – *Steve Wilkos* and *Maury Povitch*. Wilkos at least offers help and assistance to guests after they have been on the show. *Springer* and *Povitch* are strictly mob entertainment. And a mob it is. As people fight on *Springer* the mob comprising the audience screams "JERRY -- JERRY – JERRY…" The audience on *Springer* is mostly Millennials who wildly cheer for couples talking about their deviant and cheating sexual misadventures.

Today's music is no better. "Gangsta" Rap and Hip Hop promote and "sing" about violence against women, drug use, cop killing, and suicide. Not only is this garbage devastatingly loud, it shakes the ground. My family room is in the back of my house and if a car goes by on the street out front playing that noise I can feel vibrations coming through the floor. One afternoon one of our floor to ceiling glass windows suddenly shattered. We were never able to determine the cause but I suspect it was a car passing through the neighborhood playing that junk at full volume and it hit just the right pitch to shatter the windows. (That would reinforce a theory that the Israelite trumpets achieved the perfect pitch to bring down the walls of Jericho.)

This music objectifies women which encourages domestic violence and rape. It glorifies violence and we wonder why there is so much violent crime in the inner cities. It romanticizes drug use, and coarsens the language which is why we hear so much vulgarity coming out of young people in their everyday conversation. This music makes all of this seem "cool." Contrast that with the earlier (pre-late '60s) music that placed females on a pedestal and sang about genuine love and caring. This was replaced by the late '60s Heavy Metal garbage performed by drug addled "singers" but what do you expect from a band called KISS, an acronym for *Knights in Service of Satan*, perhaps the most appropriately named band of that era.

What is the state of Art when a crucifix sunk upside down in a jar of urine or an image of the Virgin Mary covered with elephant manure are both publicly (government) funded?

Our literary tradition is gone. We have no modern day Ernest Hemingway, F Scott Fitzgerald, or William Faulkner. The culture has sunk to a point where it is incapable of producing that kind of talent; if it could, it would but it isn't, so it doesn't because we have regressed too deep into *cultural immaturity*; to call this culture "adolescent" would be an insult to adolescence. It takes a sophisticated and mature culture to produce great literature, music and motion pictures.

Today's movies will not stand the test of time like *Casablanca, The Best Years of our Lives, The Ten Commandments, The Greatest Story Ever Told,* or *The Sound of Music.* Neither will today's art, music, or literature. There is no present day or recent classics in any of these categories. The occasional good movie, good song, beautiful picture and well written book get drowned in a deluge of garbage. This is a cultural catastrophe since a culture is carried forward by its literature, art, music, and screen entertainment. The only hope is that the post 1960s literature, entertainment and art have no staying power and eventually the quality products of the pre-1960s will enjoy a renaissance and inspire comparable material. If it does not, there will be nothing in these cultural categories to pass on except pornography which is the biggest business on the internet today. How's that for a statement of cultural decline?

13. *The Collapse of American Public Education (Late 1960s to the Present)*

In 1984 *A Nation at Risk* detailed the ongoing decline of the American Public School system. That was thirty years ago and things have only gotten worse. We continually rank lowest in the industrialized world in math and science. Public schools are de-emphasizing to the point of not teaching, history and civics. This is painfully evident when television programs like *Jay Leno* or the Watters World feature on *The O'Reilly Factor* and some others on You Tube go out on the street and ask random twentysomethings which countries we fought in World War II or who the vice-president is. Many just plain don't have a clue and couldn't care less by the attitudes and responses they display. Those questions are part of cultural literacy which is discouraged in favor of "diversity."

Dropout rates are high -- up to 50 percent in some inner city schools. Discipline is in shambles since teachers can no longer use corporal punishment or even speak harshly to students. But students can toss "F bombs" at teachers with little, if any, consequence. Swearing at a teacher will not even get a student suspended in the New York school district. Today teachers are routinely insulted, assaulted and groped by out-of-control students. Discipline is now regarded as racist since more Blacks get suspended for behavior issues than Whites. To deal with disciplinary problems, some school districts have adopted "restorative justice" aimed at rehabilitating students without punishment. One of the gimmicks in "restorative justice" is the "Talking Circle" where disruptive students talk out their feelings and other students and teachers are supposed to gain an "understanding" of the moron doing the talking.

"White Privilege" is another farce perpetrated by the Pacific Educational Group which has contracts with school districts in Denver, St. Louis, Seattle, St. Paul and other cities. This organization tells school districts (for a handsome fee) that minority students are disciplined and suspended at a higher rate than White students and this is discrimination. Minority students cannot be understood and dealt with in terms of "whiteness." Schools, as a result, are reluctant to discipline minority, especially Black, students and the result is predictable: out-of-control students and classrooms. It is nothing less than the racism. of lowered expectations. This is why most big city school districts are in chaos. When teachers devote most of the class period to classroom "management" instead of teaching, learning is not going to happen.

The Gresham-Barlow School district, near Portland, Oregon, contracted with the Oregon Center for Educational Equity to conduct seminars for administrators. In an on line article dated June 16, 2015, EAG.org outlined some of the material the Oregon Center for Educational Equity is disseminating: All Whites are racists whether they realize it or not; educational curricula and discipline is favors White students; Black students cannot succeed in the current educational system; personal ownership, hard work for personal gain are foreign concepts to Black students since the Black culture is collectivist in nature (the old "It takes a village" routine) thus implying that a socialist format works better for them. The public schools are being flooded with this "White Privilege" propaganda which is the racism of low expectations. Young Blacks are being indoctrinated with this nonsense in all aspects of their lives and it will only keep them stuck in the rut of poverty, crime, unemployment and underemployment. If what the Pacific Educational Group and the Oregon Center for Educational Equity say is true, why are there so many scholarships and other academic assistance programs for minorities? Maybe it is because propaganda is such a money maker for these outfits. And what about the many Blacks who do succeed and prosper in America?

In an attempt to bolster sagging achievement, the Federal Government instituted the "No Child Left Behind" program during the George W. Bush Administration. This requires students to achieve certain scores on standardized tests. This has further reduced public education to a numbers game forcing teachers to teach to the tests. This has resulted in faking test scores. In Atlanta, GA 178 teachers, principals and school employees were charged with falsifying standardized test scores for years. As a result some schools in the Atlanta District saw increases in test scores as high as 45 percent. The lead character in this scandal was Dr. Beverly Hall, Atlanta School District Superintendent who earned thousands of dollars in bonuses for raising test scores in the district. Hall was named National Superintendent of the Year in 2009 by the American Association of School Administrators for the improvement shown in the Atlanta School District during her tenure as superintendent. Teachers and principals held weekend "erasure parties" complete with delivered pizzas (probably on the District's dime) where they changed answers on standardized tests. Ten people received jail sentences while many more of those involved were fired. Hall escaped jail through death passing away from breast cancer on March 2, 2015.

High test scores bring individual teacher and administrator bonuses and are deciding factors in whether a school stays open or is closed. Millions of dollars are at stake in school districts with low test scores. Teachers feel pressured and, at least in Atlanta, they were ordered to increase scores by all means possible. Many other school districts around the country are under suspicion for rigging test scores. Atlanta is only the tip of a very large iceberg. Teaching to the test and changing scores is as destructive to the Public School system as the breakdown of discipline.

There are good school districts out there but most big city districts do not meet standards. Teachers' unions oppose any alternative such as school vouchers to help pay private school tuition, or charter schools.

Another disturbing trend today is the number of teachers accused of having sexual relations with students and it appears there are as many female teachers as male instructors involved.

The government's solution is to keep throwing money at public education but after decades of trying to resolve the problem through more dollars, we continue to miss the point. It is the lack of parental involvement, and a structured (disciplined) school environment. Much if the problem in schools can be traced to the breakdown of the family where there is little parental involvement in their children's' education either at home by making sure the kids are doing their homework and keeping up their grades or interacting and co-operating with teachers at school. Fifty years ago parents backed the school when their children were disciplined; today they are apt to sue.

Beyond all of this, we need to re-visit our philosophy of public education and start teaching to a student's individual talents. The cookie cutter approach no longer works. In my book *New Paradigms* I outline a new concept of public education that would teach to a student's abilities, aptitudes and interests. We need to return to the old basic 1-8 Elementary School where students would learn the fundamentals and then move on to a 9- 12 curriculum suited to their individual talents, interests and abilities. A curriculum of cultural literacy would be taught throughout the 12 years (including current events) since it is the duty and obligation of the schools to pass on the culture which is not happening now. Ask recent high school graduates some simple history and civics questions if you have any doubt about that.

Our current system of primary schools, elementary schools, middle schools, junior high schools and high schools are bureaucratic gimmicks designed to bring more dollars into a district and keep more teachers employed. It is a costly and ineffective system. Catholic schools still are 1-8 and 9-12 and they are producing academic excellence. The greatest beneficiaries of the current American Public School System are the millions of foreign doctors, nurses, engineers, scientists, and computer techs we have to import into this country to keep our medical facilities and technology functioning.

14. The *Technological Revolution (1980s – Present)*

The technological revolution came upon us too quickly with a constant and rapid stream of changes that many of us find difficult to absorb, especially those of us who grew up in a time of slower technological evolution. Technology eliminated many well-paying jobs once available to workers without technical expertise and higher education. This has resulted in outsourcing to foreign countries and insecure and uncertain temporary jobs and a volatile job market.

Appliances and electronics equipment -- televisions, computers, cell phones, ipods, blueberries, blackberries, tablets etc. -- all require programming (often complex) before they are operational. Some televisions require two or three remote control devices and most of us do not know what all the buttons on them do.

We are hooked on video games and mindless internet "surfing." This, along with social media and cell phones, are destroying society's capacity to interrelate and interact on a face-to-face basis. Younger people will text someone in the next room rather than walk over and speak in person. All of this creates a sense of anomie, isolation, and alienation. Young people, who carry out mass killings like Columbine and Sandy Hook, were addicted to video games and the general culture of electronic isolation.

Technology is destroying our ability to socially relate to one another. How often do we see people staring at their cell phones? If you are standing in a line most people in the line are staring blankly at cell phones. Diners in restaurants are just as often staring at some device as talking to the people sitting at the table with them. Next time you go to a movie watch what happens as people emerge into the lobby after the show is over. Nearly all of them are reaching for their "devices." When I ride the bus (nearly every day) most passengers are staring at machines. I've sat next to people on the Tacoma-Seattle bus (a 40 minute ride) who do not take their eyes off their gizmos for one minute. When I drop by Starbucks after the gym, nearly everyone in the lounge area is staring at a machine. Last week a guy had fallen asleep in one of the leather chairs, his head laying back, his hand still holding his cell phone in midair. The whole world has become an enlarged set of *The Night of the Living Dead*. Millennials would rather text than talk or if they do talk, it is on the phone. Various studies report that teens text anywhere from 60 to 100 or more times every day -- that adds up to thousands of texts per month. They live in a world of Facebook, Twitter, Instagram, Instachat, internet chat rooms, e-mail and any other kind of electronic communication that takes the place of human interaction.

Young people are committing suicide because of cyber bullying-- electronic harassment -- sometimes by people they do not know. Teen-agers especially are victimized by sexual predators that create false on line identities and set up meetings or "dates" for nefarious purposes.

This addiction to machines explains, in large part, why many younger people, and not so young people, are ill informed about current events. What news they do get is off the internet and is often unreliable or false. They do not read newspapers or listen to news on radio and television or read books. A Microsoft study found that the attention span of the average person is 8 seconds. The attention span of a goldfish is 9 seconds. The average human attention span is down from 12 seconds a decade ago and the study blames the impact of technology, the fixation with gadgets. A study by the University of Gothenburg, Sweden reveals that cell phones and computers contribute to depression and sleep issues, especially in young adults.

What will happen after two or three generations of this? Albert Einstein saw this coming decades ago and he has answered that question: ***"I fear the day that technology will surpass our human interaction. The world will have a generation of idiots."*** Or maybe it will be a generation of "human robots" with a greatly diminished capacity for human feeling.

In the workplace we are stuck in cubicles glued to a computer. Meetings, classes, training sessions and hosts of other activities that used to be in a group setting with group interaction have been replaced by a single person sitting at a computer listening to disconnected voices or simply reading impersonal text. Human beings need that personal interaction face-to-face, one-on-one or in groups, that technology has taken away from us. When you call Customer Service you often have to go through a "virtual receptionist" -- a disembodied mechanical voice that tries to sound human while driving you nuts. Sometimes you can say (or scream in frustration) "AGENT" and be transferred to someone in India or the Philippines, but not always.

Technology is in constant flux and change. Today's state-of-the-art computer, printer, cell phone or whatever are tomorrow's dinosaurs and this has spilled over into the culture at large. It is socially unhealthy when we cannot depend on consistency and stability or at least a slower pace of development. This does not rule out change but the changes I experienced growing up in the 1950s came at a pace easy to absorb and were uncomplicated and easy to learn. Technology has made society so complex that it takes a high level of training and intelligence to be able to navigate through it and know enough to make an adequate living with it. Jobs that were simple and uncomplicated a few years ago now require a high level of computer knowledge. "Unskilled" jobs are disappearing and that means more people will not be able to make a living wage. When I retired I only half-facetiously remarked that the Washington State employment application had gotten so complex that I couldn't qualify for Janitor 1.

Technology controls our lives. If there were a computer meltdown on the level some feared would occur when the calendar rolled over to the year 2000 (Y2K)* society would descend into chaos and anarchy since we would not be able to perform the simplest tasks. EVERYTHING is tied into computers. A worldwide, or even nationwide, computer disaster could literally knock us back to the days before electricity because all electrical systems run by computer. As I was reviewing this chapter, all the computers at a local Walmart crashed. All business came to a complete halt. People got tired of waiting and walked out of the store leaving full shopping carts sitting in the aisles. Some people had some of their merchandise charged before the system went down. On July 8, 2015, the New York Stock Exchange, the Wall Street Journal home page, and United Airlines all suffered computer glitches that temporarily shut down the NYSE and grounded United flights. Coincidence or perhaps a dry run for a bigger hit down the road?

We are totally dependent on technology and total dependence on any kind of material entity means that we are one step away from a catastrophe. Several nations have capability to emit electromagnetic pulses that could knock out our power grid. This could paralyze the electronic infrastructure of part or all of the country. So could a major solar flare for that matter. In 1859 there was a solar flare that knocked out the telegraph system for a while. Since homes and businesses functioned without electricity at that time, it had no effect on most of the country. Today it would bring us to our knees. The United States would become a real life post-apocalyptic *Mad Max* style movie.

It's not a question of IF, rather a question of WHEN some hostile country or terrorist organization figures out how to hit the delete button on our entire technological infrastructure. Our computer systems are vulnerable to hacking. Major corporations are always announcing that they've been hacked and millions of customers' account information including Social Security numbers and credit card information have been "compromised." Not long ago China hacked into a federal computer network and stole private information on at least four million Federal Government employees. Those who worship at the altar of technology may someday sacrifice everything to that false god.

*

(AUTHOR'S NOTE: Y2K or Year 2000 -- the letter K being an alpha symbol for 1000 -- was based on the fear that when the calendar rolled over to the year 2000 all computer functions would abruptly cease since many computers were programmed with a 2 digit year e.g., July 1, 1999 read 070199. So January 1, 2000 would read 010100 making the computer "think" that we had gone back to 1900. Many computer experts believed that there would be a worldwide system crash -- airplanes would fall out of the sky, public utilities would shut down, the world financial system would collapse etc. So there was a mad scramble to re-program all computer systems with 4 digit years. It was a hollow panic.)

15. *The Rise of Political Correctness and Multiculturalism(1970s to Present)*

This is a two part cultural choke point that rates separate chapters because it is not only a choke point but it is a key factor in the destruction of our culture. See chapters 6 and 7..

16. *The Clinton Presidency (1993-2001)*

This was a cultural choke point because, for the first time, Americans were willing to accept inappropriate personal behavior in a national leader. Bill Clinton's presidency was cluttered by accusations from several women of sexual harassment including an allegation of rape. These occurred before he became president while he was Governor of Arkansas but they were public knowledge during his first presidential campaign. During his second term in the White House he had an affair with a White House intern, Monica Lewinski. This was an oral sex relationship with her that took place in the Oval Office itself. He lied about it under oath and this initiated impeachment proceedings.

He dodged being thrown out of office and his popularity increased with the American public. People didn't care anymore about the moral character of the president; in fact, his increasing popularity implied indirect public approval of his immorality. Contrast this with the Adlai Stevenson divorce issue in the 1952 and 1956 presidential elections. Some historians believe this was a deciding factor in Stevenson losing these elections. People remarked about Stevenson at the time: "If you can't manage your home, how can you manage the country?" Had the public been made aware of John F. Kennedy's prolific sexual activities he would never have been elected and if they had come to light during his presidency it may have brought about impeachment; at the very least he never would have been able to even consider a second term.

Public morality has declined precipitously since the Kennedy era. Clinton was all but applauded for his moral failings since they mirrored the cultural morality of his time. The economy was doing well and in the materialistic society that we had become, that was all that mattered. Clinton was Everyman. He was one of us because so many of us were doing what he was doing and we loved him for it. There was absolutely no criticism of Clinton from the Feminists about the Lewinsky affair or any of the other allegations. As long as he supported abortion they would stand "shoulder to shoulder" with him according to National Organization of Women Pesident, Patricia Ireland.

17. *Same SexMarriage (2004-Present)*

In April 2004 San Francisco Mayor, Gavin Newsome, authorized marriage licenses for Gay and Lesbian couples living in the city. Newsome acted in clear violation of California State law but there were no repercussions and no action from then Governor Arnold Schwarzenegger who later came out as personally favoring same sex marriage. At the same time, the Massachusetts Supreme Court declared same sex marriage legal in that state. Seattle Mayor, Greg Nichols said he would recognize same sex marriages contracted in other states. Washington State legalized same sex marriage in 2012 by decree of the State Legislature. It was later affirmed by the voters of Washinton State in a ballot initiative. Same sex marriage became legal in all 50 States by a decision of the U.S. Supreme Court on June 26, 2015. It is also legal in 24 European countries.

.

In 1996 President Clinton (of all people) signed into Federal Law the Defense of Marriage Act (DOMA) that declared marriage as being between one man and one woman under Federal law. In 2013 the United States Supreme Court declared DOMA unconstitutional.

So what is wrong with same sex marriage beyond the religious objections and what makes it a cultural choke point? There are four points to consider:

(1) It provides a slippery slope for polygamy and polyandry. There is both biblical and historical precedent for polygamy. Polyandry (one woman, multiple husbands) has been practiced around the world mostly in primitive societies. Polygamy is currently legal in Muslim countries. The Mormons practiced it here in the United States until the Federal Government stepped in and prohibited it during the late 19th century. There is no longer a valid argument against polygamy and polyandry since we have legalized same sex marriage, something for which there is no historical precedent. We historically defined marriage in the United States as the union of one man and one woman. We have now re-defined it. Why can't we re-define it again -- and again?

(2) The human anatomy is not designed for same gender sex. Ever try plugging two male or two female hose ends together? It doesn't work. Until the 1970s, the American Psychiatric Association defined homosexuality as an abnormality. Political Correctness changed that.

(3) Same sex marriage is based totally on emotional arguments --not logic; and if it is a "right", why do you need a license to get married? Like driving, marriage is a privilege, not a right. It would be easier to argue for civil unions as a right and leave marriage in the religious realm -- up to the churches.

(4) Same sex marriage is having a detrimental effect on marriage because it dilutes marriage. Marriage has traditionally been between a man and a woman. If anyone can do it, then what makes it so special? It will have the same effect that co-habitation has had on marriage. Like, why bother? As we mentioned earlier, 2013 registered the lowest number of marriages to date.

Since same sex marriage became the norm in Europe, the marriage rate has declined over there. Therein may be the real purpose of same sex marriage. The following news release seems to support that assertion:

May 1, 2013 (LifeSiteNews.com) – Conservative pundits are saying that a homosexual activist exposed the hidden agenda behind homosexual 'marriage' when she told an audience last year that the movement is not seeking equality but rather a total dismantling of the institution of marriage itself.

Masha Gessen, a journalist and author who campaigns for homosexual 'rights', made the comments last May in Australia on a panel at the Sydney Writer's Festival. She said:

"It's a no-brainer that (homosexual activists) should have the right to marry, but I also think equally that it's a no-brainer that the institution of marriage should not exist. Fighting for gay marriage generally involves lying about what we are going to do with marriage when we get there — because we lie that the institution of marriage is not going to change, and that is a lie.

"The institution of marriage is going to change, and it should change. And again, I don't think it should exist. And I don't like taking part in creating fictions about my life. That's sort of not what I had in mind when I came out thirty years ago."

Providing her own life as an example for her advocacy to do away with marriage, Gessen described the complex family structure in which three children whom she parents live: one of them is adopted with her ex-partner, another - whom she birthed – has a biological father in Russia, and the third is the biological child of her current partner and Gessen's brother. These three children have five adults in parenting roles, but not all five adults parent all three children.

The five parents break down into two groups of three," she said. "And really, I would like to live in a legal system that is capable of reflecting that reality, and I don't think that's compatible with the institution of marriage."

(End of article)

Traditional marriage has been the bulwark of every society because it is the legal and legitimate means of procreation that keeps the society going from generation to generation. The ideal family is designed to provide both a male and a female role model. Some same sex couples may adopt children. Two Gay men will never procreate their own child and a Lesbian couple will often do so via artificial insemination. All of this runs contrary to the philosophy of marriage and same sex marriage will diminish traditional marriage both in cultural importance and number.

On June 26, 2015 the United States Supreme Court in a 6-3 decision declared same sex marriage legal in all fifty States. This is in direct violation of the Tenth Amendment to the United States Constitution which states that the Federal Government has authority only in what is specifically allowed to it under the Constitution; the rest is delegated to the states and to the people. Marriage is not a Constitutional right; it is a privilege requiring a license and permission by *State* jurisdiction, not Federal. This is another indication of cultural decline, not only in the disintegration of marriage but in the increasingly totalitarian control the Federal Government is exercising over the American people.

Same sex marriage, like abortion, is cultural rather than constitutional. The Supreme Court decisions legalizing both abortion and same sex marriage were based upon the culture -- not the Constitution since there is no provision in the Constitution that grants federal jurisdiction over procreation or marriage. The Court may have put a constitutional "spin" on their decisions cloaking them in "legalese" but the decisions were constructed on a cultural foundation, not a constitutional foundation.

Culture has trumped the Constitution in the past with the Dred Scott decision (1857) which decreed that Black Americans could not be American citizens, and Plessy vs Ferguson (1896) that made segregation ("Separate but Equal") the law of the land. These decisions discriminated against Blacks because of the culture at the time, not the Constitution. Supreme Court decisions are influenced by the culture (and that applies to many political decisions as well). Supreme Court decisions and Federal laws will change when the culture changes as we saw when slavery and segregation lost cultural favor. Brown vs Board of Education (1954) overturned Plessy vs Ferguson in Public Education by de-segregating public schools. Abortion and same sex marriage will not be revoked until the culture changes. Lawmaking in a democratic society is based on cultural norms and trends although no one will admit that.

(AUTHOR'S NOTE: All societal functions need to be judged and evaluated based on their primary purpose. The primary purpose of marriage is the continuation of the society in an orderly and structured fashion. It is larger than human emotions and feelings which is what same sex marriage is all about. If Gays and Lesbians want to live together that is between them and the Deity. I would be in favor of civil unions that would allow them to manage finances and property in common. Society should leave them alone; in other words, no anti-sodomy laws. But traditional marriage is the glue that holds the culture and society together and, as we have discussed above, same sex marriage will only serve to dilute the institution of marriage just as co-habitation and the increasing divorce rate have done already.

No society that allows for abortion, same sex marriage, and physician assisted suicide (see below) and legalized drugs can be a great society since these dysfunctions lead to narcissism that stunts and diminishes the continued growth and development of that society.)

There is also a religious freedom issue here. Businesses that refuse to cater same sex weddings face civil prosecution. As I write this, Melissa and Aaron Klein, owners of a bakery in Gresham, Oregon, were ordered by the Court to pay $135000.00 in damages for refusing to bake a cake for a same sex wedding. There have been other cases like this and the legal system does not recognize freedom of conscience in them. These businesses have clearly stated that they have no problem serving Gays and Lesbians but they will not cater same sex weddings since it runs contrary to their religious beliefs. This has the potential to become a major problem as militant Gay organizations will deliberately target Christian businesses and try to destroy them with lawsuits and civil action.

In Kentucky, Rowan County Clerk, Kim Davis, was sentenced to jail for Contempt of Court for refusing to issue marriage licenses to same sex couples after a judge ordered her to do so. Same sex marriage could be the catalyst for religious persecution in the United States.

(AUTHOR'S NOTE: The Churches -- both Protestant and Catholic -- are so far, conspicuous by their absence. Why aren't they openly defending people like Kim Davis and the business owners who are being prosecuted and persecuted for their religious beliefs?)

The Left tries to float the argument that religious reasons were used to oppose interracial marriages in the past. This is true -- however, that was an erroneous (intentional or unintentional) theory. Interracial marriage is not mentioned anywhere in Scripture. Homosexuality is and it is condemned in no uncertain terms.

18. *Physician Assisted Suicide. (Late 1990s to present)*

Physician Assisted Suicide started in Europe but is growing in popularity in the United States. As of July 2015, Physician Assisted Suicide is legal in 5 states -- Washington, Oregon, Montana, New Mexico and Vermont. In Europe it is legal in the Netherlands, Germany, Belgium, Luxembourg, Albania, and Switzerland. It is also legal in Colombia and Japan. It is the next level down on the slippery slope that began with the advent of the Birth Control pill in 1960, followed by the legalization of abortion in 1973. Physician assisted suicide began gaining traction in the 1990s. The following article by Ronald D. Rotunda in the April 27, 2015 article in *Verdict p*resents one of the best summaries of this cultural choke point that I have yet seen. Once again, all we need to do is look to Europe to see where this is heading. It ratchets up pop dropping and granny dumping to new levels beyond simply warehousing them in a nursing home.

The Way of Death in the Netherlands, Oregon, and, Perhaps, California
By Ronald Rotunda

Four states (when this article was written) now approve of doctor-assisted suicide. A bill recently introduced in the California Senate SB 128, the so-called "The End of Life Option Act," would make California the fifth state. As medical science has progressed, we can extend life. Some people think that, at some point, the doctors are not prolonging life but only prolonging death. Hence, groups like the Hemlock Society say that they seek a "right to die" or "death with compassion."

In 1997, the U.S. Supreme Court held, in Washington v. Glucksberg and in Vacco v. Quill, that there is no constitutional right to suicide. However, both decisions repeatedly reaffirmed that under the law in every state, we already have a right to painkillers, even though the painkillers may in some cases also have an effect of hastening death. Similarly, under existing law, people have the right to refuse treatment that they regard as excessive or overly burdensome. In Cruzan v. Director, Missouri Department of Health, Chief Justice Rehnquist said that it "cannot be disputed that the Due Process Clause protects the interest in life as well as an interest in refusing life-sustaining medical treatment." That, by the way, is also the position of religious groups like the Catholic Church. What we already have a right to do—refuse treatment, accept painkillers, write living wills, enter hospice—all that is quite different from what the proposed California bill would authorize.

We have learned a lot about doctor-assisted suicide over the years. How it begins and what it becomes. For example, in the spring of 2001, the Netherlands had completely decriminalized euthanasia and doctor-assisted suicide. However, even before that, medical practice accepted euthanasia and Dutch prosecutors found it almost impossible to win cases because of a series of court rulings. When the prosecutors did win, courts suspended the sentences of the doctors. Public opinion polls showed that 80 percent of Dutch citizens favored voluntary euthanasia.

Dutch governmental reports show that in 1990, of the 130,000 Dutch who died, about 11,800 died because they were "killed or helped to die by their doctors. In slightly over half of these cases, the doctors did not have their patients' consent. Another Dutch survey is particularly interesting. In a survey of the elderly that did not mention euthanasia (no leading questions here), more than 10 percent volunteered that they feared being put to sleep by their doctors if they went to a Dutch hospital. When Dutch doctors consider assisting suicide, the guidelines tell them to look at the "loneliness," "financial resources," and a "loss of social skills" of their patients.

In the Netherlands, euthanasia extends to terminally ill children, disabled infants, and mental patients. In 1997, The Lancet, a British medical journal, reported that eight percent of infants who die in the Netherlands were "put to sleep" by their doctors. In 1993, the Dutch Pediatric Society issued guidelines for killing infants. The Royal Dutch Society for Pharmacology helpfully sends a book to all new doctors with formulas for poisons to induce euthanasia.

It was not always so. Hitler issued his first direct order for euthanasia on October 1, 1939 (backdated to September 1). Those orders spread to all the Nazi-occupied countries. Ten years later, in 1949, a New England Journal of Medicine article reported that during World War II, Dutch doctors—unlike the doctors of every other Nazi-occupied country—did not participate in even one act of euthanasia. Nuremburg condemned euthanasia as a war crime. The view of Dutch doctors changed. As Malcolm Muggeridge, the British journalist, observed, "it took no more than three decades to transfer a war crime into an act of compassion."

Belgium officially approved doctor-assisted suicide in 2002. Last year, it removed all age restrictions on euthanasia. From 2002 to 2014, the number of euthanasia cases increased nearly 6,000 percent. Last year, over 1,400 people were euthanatized. Some doctors talk of assisted suicide together with organ transplants. The first reported case of organ harvesting of an assisted suicide patient in Belgium was in 2008. Since then, Belgium has harvested organs from euthanized patients who are mentally ill. The number of assisted suicides that doctors and nurses report do not reflect the actual number of assisted suicides. The British Medical Journal reported in 2010 that in Flanders alone, the actual reported assisted suicides are only about 50 percent of the actual number of assisted suicides.

The Canadian Medical Association studied assisted suicides in Belgium and found that about half of the euthanasia deaths were not voluntary. In some cases, nurses, not doctors, made the final decision. Belgium law does not approve of "non-voluntary assisted suicide" (an oxymoron) but the government rarely enforces that law. Like other European countries, it has socialized medicine, and assisted suicide helps reduce costs.

The Swiss Federal Supreme Court declared, in 2006, that the mentally ill have a "right" to assisted suicide. One American commentator rejoiced with the argument of the court that "we are entering an era during which psychiatric patients do not need to be protected, but empowered." If you think that psychiatric patients do not need protection, then assisted suicide is the way to go. One should not conclude that Switzerland is heartless just because its courts conclude that it does not need to protect its mentally ill citizens. Switzerland, a very civilized country, makes it illegal to catch and release fish because that is inhumane. The Swiss also ban using live bait for fishing because that is also inhumane.

The Netherlands, Belgium, Switzerland—these countries find that assisted suicide is a slippery slope. It won't happen here, you say. Well, Oregon legalized assisted suicide in 1994. In 2008, it sponsored a health plan that denied recommended cancer treatments that were costly; instead, it offered to pay for less-expensive suicide drugs. Oregon told patient Barbara Wagner that it would not pay for the new chemotherapy drug Tarceva, which her doctor recommended could add years to her life. The Oregon state official "admitted they must consider the state's limited dollars when dealing with a case such as Wagner's." ABC News reported that a 1998 study of the Georgetown University Center for Clinical Bioethics "found a strong link between cost-cutting pressures on physicians and their willingness to prescribe lethal drugs to patients—were it legal to do so."

A 1998 article in the New England Journal of Medicine estimated that "legalizing physician-assisted suicide and euthanasia would save Medicare approximately $627 million in 1995 dollars." As Dr. Paul McHugh, the former psychiatrist in chief at Johns Hopkins Hospital, concluded after studying our experiences with assisted suicide, "When a 'right to die' becomes settled law, soon the right translates into a duty."

Proponents of the proposed California law say it can't happen here. California is not Oregon. On the other hand, listen to what Justice John Paul Stevens said in his dissent in Cruzan. The Court refused to interfere with Missouri law regarding living wills. Stevens complained that "it is an effort to define life rather than protect it, that is the heart of Missouri's policy." What is wrong is that "Missouri insists" on "equating [Nancy Cruzan's] life with the biological persistence of her bodily functions."

That solves the problem nicely, doesn't it? We simply redefine "life" to mean something more than just "life." It must be a full, worthwhile life. We can adopt the Dutch guidelines, and look at the "loneliness," "financial resources," and a "loss of social skills" of patients. If they fail the test, they are not really alive, although they continue to burden society by not dying.

Marilyn Golden, of the Disability Rights Education and Defense Fund, rejects that line of reasoning and opposes assisted suicide. Speaking on behalf of the disabled, she warns: This fear of disability typically underlies assisted suicide. Said one assisted suicide advocate, "Pain is not the main reason we want to die. It's the indignity. It's the inability to get out of bed or get onto the toilet . . . [People] . . . say, 'I can't stand my mother—my husband—wiping my behind.' It's about dignity." But as many thousands of people with disabilities who rely on personal assistance have learned, needing help is not undignified, and death is not better than reliance on assistance. Have we gotten to the point that we will abet suicides because people need help using the toilet?

(End of article)

(AUTHOR'S NOTE: Physician assisted suicide re-defines life just as same sex marriage re-defines marriage. Also, it is only a matter of time when family members will be allowed to make that decision for their relatives and you can be sure financial considerations will come into play just as much as misguided "compassion.")

19. *Drug Legalization (2012-Present)*

Washington State and Colorado legalized marijuana by popular vote in 2012 in clear violation of Federal Law. The states put in myriads of regulations governing, sales and amounts, growing and selling. Sales were limited to adults 21 and over. Implementation turned out to be more complicated than supporters realized in their initial high over legalization.

The choke point here is that drug usage, once heavily penalized under the law, is now socially acceptable and legal. Millennials smoke marijuana like Baby Boomers and other generations smoked cigarettes. Supporters of legalization can cite studies proving that marijuana smoking is less hazardous than cigarettes while opponents cite just as many studies to the contrary. Secular Progressives, who treat cigarette smoking like rendering the Hitler salute or waving the Confederate flag, champion marijuana smoking. This is largely due to their 1960s upbringing. They can legitimately state the dangers of cigarette smoking and alcohol abuse but, as we said earlier, the goal of marijuana is to get high. You can have a couple of drinks and not get drunk but one joint puts you in rapid ascent mode.

Drugs destroy communities and lives. Most of today's crime is driven by drugs. Legalizing drugs will not lower the crime rate because people commit crimes when they are _on_ drugs. Drugs are mind altering. And here again we have the slippery slope -- marijuana today, cocaine and heroin tomorrow. No culture can function when a significant percentage of the population uses drugs (including marijuana) on a regular basis. You can see the effects of drug usage in major urban downtown areas -- high rates of violent crime. Drugs are a driving factor in homelessness. A culture with easy and legal access to drugs is a dysfunctional society because drugs facilitate and drive dysfunctional behavior.

Marijuana does have some medicinal benefits. It helps patients with multiple sclerosis and some other illnesses and mitigates the side effects oc chemotherapy. If marijuana, or any other drug, can ease pain and negative side effects, it should be prescribed and dispensed through regular pharmacies just like any other medication. Medical marijuana stores are a travesty. If marijuana is legitimately prescribed, dispense it in the conventional manner.

20. _The Re-election of President Barack Obama (2012)_

We are talking about the re-election of President Obama rather than his first election in 2008. He was elected in 2008 in the wake of the financial meltdown in the mortgage and banking industries that led to the worst financial crisis since the Great Depression. That and two unpopular wars (Afghanistan and Iraq) virtually ensured a Democratic win in 2008. Even then it was close (52-48).

The problem with Obama's re-election was his first term record. He added $6 trillion to the national Debt during his first term in office. Obama ran four consecutive trillion dollar deficits. He enacted a $787 billion stimulus package that did absolutely nothing to stimulate the economy. He also pushed through a government controlled healthcare mandate that is loaded with hidden taxes, fees, and fines and governed by (as of this writing) 13,000 pages of regulations that no one person completely understands. The Affordable Healthcare Act (aka Obamacare) has never enjoyed majority approval from the American Public. Unemployment remained at over 8 percent until the last two months of his first term when it dipped to 7.8 percent.

His foreign policy was a shambles.   Iran grew as a threat in the Middle East throughout his first term as they continued their progress toward developing nuclear weapons.. Relations with Israel are at their lowest point since Israel became a nation in 1947. Obama supported the Muslim Brotherhood government of Mohammed Morsi in Egypt, an avowed enemy of Israel, after abandoning long time American ally, President Hosni Mubarak. Obama did nothing to support what could have been a popular grassroots uprising in Iran that could have potentially led to the overthrow of that anti-American regime in power since 1979.

Obama's foreign policy is a major choke point in itself since it has ended American leadership in the world. This began during his first term and is accelerating in his second term. Complaints about the United States being "the world's policeman" date back to the 1950s but the 20th century made it clear that only American leadership can preserve global stability and effectively stop potential conquerors. American intervention and leadership defeated Nazi Germany and Imperial Japan. Europe was a player but not a leader in the war and it could not have prevailed without the United States. United States leadership saved South Korea from conquest by North Korea and Communist China. The Korean War was officially a United Nations War but American leadership won it. American Leadership prevented Soviet Russia from taking over Europe during the immediate post-war years. American Leadership contained Soviet expansionism and eventually put an end to the Soviet Union. American leadership stopped Iraq under Saddam Hussein from taking over the Persian Gulf oil fields in 1990 by putting together a multi-nation coalition of nations from the Middle East, Europe, Asia and Africa.

American leadership had Al Qaida on the ropes. Obama ended all of that with his "strategy" of leading from behind. The Middle East is in chaos with ISIS dominating much of Syria and Iraq and Iran expanding its influence throughout the region at the same time. Terrorism has spread into Africa. Hundreds of thousands of refugees from the Middle East and Africa are crossing the Mediterranean into Europe creating the worst refugee and humanitarian crisis since World War II. This crisis has the potential to destabilize Europe since it already is overrun with Muslim immigrants. Even before Middle Eastern refugees began pouring into Europe, Christians were being slaughtered by the thousands in Syria and Iraq while we did nothing for them either. All of this could have been prevented by early, quick and decisive action under American leadership. Much of it could have been prevented if Obama had left a residual force of American ground troops in Iraq.

Russia is expanding into the Ukraine and threatening the Baltic States. China is threatening countries in the Far East with its expansionism in the South China Sea.

ISIS, Iran, Russia and China know that Obama will do nothing except try to appease them. An America acting as a world leader would have galvanized the Middle East and destroyed ISIS, would never have signed the Iranian nuclear arms agreement which effectively gives it a pathway to the bomb. This will encourage other countries in the region to "nuke up." We should have kept the economic sanctions in place against Iran but now the genie is out of the bottle and other countries are rushing in to do business with Iran thereby strengthening its position in the Middle East to promote terrorism. Saudi Arabia is turning to Russia for weapons since they know that they cannot count on the United States.

A proactive America would have armed the Ukraine, increased our military presence in Eastern Europe and never would have dismantled the missile defense system we had set up in Eastern Europe. We would have a naval presence in the South China Sea performing joint military exercises with our allies in that region.

There is no place on earth that can honestly and realistically call itself secure. No other free country has the strength and the resources to lead and this has been the case since 1940. World security rises and falls in direct proportion to the rise and fall of global American leadership.

Obama has destroyed the Global Order that had been in place since World War II and the disastrous consequences are increasing exponentially.

The economic recovery after the 2008 crash never really took off. The median wage fell by $2500.00 during his first term. Two million more citizens now live in poverty and the Black poverty rate is up by one and a half percent since Obama first took office. Unemployment in real numbers has always been over 10 percent. Unemployment rates are calculated by how many people are currently drawing Unemployment benefits. When a claimant's benefits expire they are no longer counted as unemployed even if they do not have a job. So Unemployment statistics are misleading. Many, if not most, new jobs today are part time (under 40 hours per week).

So how did Barack Obama get re-elected? His opponent, Mitt Romney, had a proven track record as a highly successful private sector manager and business owner as well as a successful term as governor of Massachusetts -- one of the strongest Democratic states in the country. The answer can be found in exit poll answers. Many believed Romney was more capable of handling the financial problems facing the country but Obama "cares more about us." Much of this perception was the Obama campaign's successful portrayal of Romney as a heartless capitalist. The most blatant example of this was a TV campaign ad featuring a man who claimed he had lost his job due to Romney's brutal business practices. This caused him to lose his health insurance and, as a result, his wife died from cancer. The truth is that when he got laid off he was carried on his wife's employee policy. When she got laid off they lost their health insurance and that's when she developed cancer. His wife's employer had no connection with Romney.

But the reason goes deeper yet. Historically, the electorate was steeped in the traditional American values of self-reliance and limited government. The growing Asian, Hispanic, and Black demographics come from an "it takes a village" culture. The Obama campaign successfully appealed to their fears that the Republicans were going to take away Entitlements and ruthlessly destroy immigrant families through mass deportations. None of this was true but the mental image was planted. In an increasingly complex and uncertain society, people wanted the reassurance that someone was going to take care of them and make certain nothing would happen to hurt them or their families. This fear was rooted in a large percentage of the White community as well as the minorities. Life is more complex today. Jobs paying living family wages that do not require much education are no longer available. People without high school diplomas and a fair amount of computer knowledge will not earn a living family wage in today's economy. People are scared and they want a benevolent caregiver government that will give them "Stuff." So never mind Obama's abysmal first term performance record. As long as the government Entitlements are coming through, all is well. Self-interest has replaced self-reliance because self-reliance has become a frightening concept in today's world.

This fear factor is most likely going to assure another Democratic presidential victory in 2016. The Republicans represent an America that is disappearing and being replaced by an America that wants government to take care of everyone. The Republicans cannot successfully counter this phenomenon.

Most people do not understand the gravity of the National Debt and they have no conception of the importance of a viable strategic foreign policy to America's national security. The public cannot grasp that what happens in other parts of the world will eventually have a direct effect on us here at home. They didn't in the 1930s which allowed Nazi Germany and Imperial Japan to pose a direct threat to the United States. The American people have become disconnected from what happens beyond their own lives and interests. Instead of keeping informed about national and international events, they are immersed in Facebook, Twitter and other social media. They are uninformed so they make uninformed choices. This is especially true of Millennials, one of the largest voting blocs. They are too involved and immersed in their gadgets and so are the least informed.

The re-election of Barack Obama underscores that America has now become an Entitlement based society with increasingly liberal social attitudes. His first term was worse than Jimmy Carter's (1977-1981) and Carter was buried in the Reagan landslide. Reagan carried states that would be impossible for a Republican to win today because we were not Entitlement minded and as socially liberal or as culturally diverse as we are now. When Reagan was elected, abortion was a major issue but same sex marriage, physician assisted suicide and legalized drugs were not even under discussion. Race relations were nowhere near as volatile as they are today.

Entitlements and divisive social issues have totally changed our political and cultural landscape which works in favor of the Democratic Party that has no permanent philosophy and simply goes with the cultural flow. When it seemed politically opportune, Barack Obama supported traditional marriage. When it became clear the tide was turning he switched his position and was never challenged for it in the mainstream press which also supports same sex marriage.

The 2012 election showed that the Republicans, with their support for traditional values, self-reliance, limited government, personal accountability and a Free Market economy are becoming out-of-touch with a population that is becoming more inclined toward the European Social Democratic model with cradle to grave entitlements combined with a growing cultural rejection of Judeo-Christian morality. Our votes are now based more on individual interests and emotion than on the Common Good and logic which defined pre-1960s America. We may have reached a point in our historical evolution where it is culturally impossible for a conservative traditionalist to win the presidency.

(AUTHOR'S NOTE: More cultural choke points will emerge as the culture continues to decline.)

+++

The choke points cited above are specific to the United States. But there are 15 general indicators of cultural decay that always appear when a culture is in decline.

1. Decline of religious practice and observance.
2. Decline of the traditional family into single parent, fragmented, alternative lifestyles and dysfunctional families. This dysfunction is often rooted in drugs, alcohol and various forms of abuse – physical and psychological.
3. Widespread public ignorance of a culture's history, traditions and values.
4. A significant disconnect between generations making it difficult to transmit a culture's history, traditions and values.

5. An increasing feeling of anomie and isolation and the loss of the sense of community.

6. Two or three generations in which no, or very little, quality literature, music, art and motion pictures are created. These venues now cater to the lowest cultural denominators.

7. A preoccupation and obsession with sex that spills over into all cultural vehicles (books, music, television and movies).

8. Decline in the practice and respect for traditional values -- honesty, personal responsibility, integrity ("My word is my bond"), sexual morality, and a strong work ethic. A good example of this is the growing number of irresponsible young men who procreate children then abandon and refuse to support them or the mothers of these children.

9. A marked increase in moral dysfunction -- extramarital sex, abortion, pedophilia and child abuse, divorce, suicide, open homosexuality, domestic violence and a growing public acceptance, or at least toleration, of these dysfunctions.

10. A declining public education system.

11. A growing sense that "the country owes me" (Entitlement mentality).

12. Coarseness and vulgarity of language in the society at large as well as in books, music and movies.

13. A growing lack of respect for life (abortion and physician assisted suicide). Human beings become disposable commodities.

14. A lack of respect for older members of society and reluctance to draw upon their wisdom and experience.

15. Decline of patriotism which is sometimes replaced with dislike for one's own country.

Chapter 6

Political Correctness

Political Correctness (PC) is a speech code designed to protect "people of color" minorities, women. LBGTs, PR actioners of non-western religions, people with disabilities or perceived disabilities, and any other approved member group in The Society of the Perpetually Offended from speech that may cause them feelings of angst, distress, inferiority or any other negative emotion. Politically Incorrect is anything that is Traditional (conservative) -- Christian, Jewish, or White male. Political Correctness is a religious dogma of sorts that substitutes for the religious dogma that the Secular Progressives want to destroy and replace.

The following is from an article titled "19 Shocking Examples of How Political Correctness is Destroying America" by Michael Snyder that appeared in *Right Side News* on August 14, 2013.

If you say the "wrong thing" in America today, you could be penalized, fired or even taken to court. Political correctness is running rampant, and it is absolutely destroying this nation. In his novel *1984*, George Orwell imagined a future world where speech was greatly restricted. He called that language that the totalitarian state in his novel created "Newspeak", and it bears a striking resemblance to the political correctness that we see in America right now. According to Wikipedia, Newspeak is "a reduced language created by the totalitarian state as a tool to limit free thought, and concepts that pose a threat to the regime such as freedom, self-expression, individuality, peace, etc. Any form of thought alternative to the party's construct is classified as 'thoughtcrime.'" Yes, people are not usually being hauled off to prison for what they are saying just yet, but we are heading down that path. Every single day, the mainstream media in the United States bombards us with subtle messages about what we should believe and what "appropriate speech" consists of. Most of the time, most Americans quietly fall in line with this unwritten speech code. In fact, most of the time we enforce this unwritten speech code among each other. Those that would dare to buck the system are finding out that the consequences can be rather severe. The following are 19 shocking examples of how political correctness is destroying America…

#1 The Missouri State Fair has permanently banned a rodeo clown from performing just because he wore an Obama mask, and now all of the other rodeo clowns are being required to take "sensitivity training" …

But the state commission went further, saying it will require that before the Rodeo Cowboy Association can take part in any future state fair, "they must provide evidence to the director of the Missouri State Fair that they have proof that all officials and subcontractors of the MRCA have successfully participated in sensitivity training.

(AUTHOR'S NOTE: Would the reaction have been the same if the clown had been wearing a Bush mask, a Reagan mask or a Sarah Palin mask? You can say or do just about anything if it is directed toward someone out of favor with the molders of opinion -- the media, academics and entertainment industry.)

#2 Government workers in Seattle have been told that they should no longer use the words "citizen" and "brown bag" because they are potentially offensive.

#3 A Florida police officer recently lost his job for calling Trayvon Martin a "thug" on Facebook.

#4 "Climate change deniers" are definitely not wanted at the U.S. Department of the Interior. Interior Secretary Sally Jewell was recently quoted as making the following statement: "I hope there are no climate-change deniers in the Department of Interior"**. (AUTHOR'S NOTE: Rhode Island Senator Sheldon Whitehouse would like to charge climate change deniers with federal conspiracy charges under the RICO Act.)**

#5 A professor at Ball State University was recently banned from even mentioning the concept of intelligent design because it would supposedly "violate the academic integrity" of the course that he was teaching.

#6 The mayor of Washington D.C. recently asked singer Donnie McClurkin <u>not to attend his own concert</u> because of his views on homosexuality.

#7 U.S. Senator Chuck Schumer is calling on athletes marching in the opening ceremonies at the Winter Olympics in Sochi next year to "<u>embarrass</u>" Russian President Vladimir Putin by protesting for gay rights.

#8 Chaplains in the U.S. military <u>are being forced</u> to perform gay marriages, even if it goes against their personal religious beliefs. The few chaplains that have refused to follow orders know that it means the end of their careers.

   (AUTHOR'S NOTE: The Government considered this but backed off when they realized they would lose all of their Roman Catholic chaplains and many chaplains from other faiths as well -- especially Muslim chaplains.)

#9 The governor of California <u>has signed a bill into law</u> which will allow transgendered students to use whatever bathrooms and gym facilities that they would like…

   Transgendered students in California will now have the right to use whichever bathrooms they prefer and join either the boys' or girls' sports teams, thanks to landmark legislation signed by Democratic Gov. Jerry Brown on Monday.

   The law <u>amends</u> the state's education code, and stipulates that each student will have access to facilities, sports teams, and programs that are "consistent with his or her gender identity," rather than the student's actual biological composition. A male student who self-identifies as female could therefore use the girls' bathroom, even if he is anatomically male.

#10 In San Francisco, authorities have installed small plastic "<u>privacy screens</u>" on library computers so that perverts can continue to exercise their "right" to watch pornography at the library without children being directly exposed to it.

#11 In America today, there are many groups that are absolutely obsessed with <u>eradicating every mention of God</u> out of the public sphere. For example, an elementary school in North Carolina ordered a little six-year-old girl to remove the word "God" from a poem that she wrote to honor her two grandfathers that had served in the Vietnam War.

#12 A high school track team was disqualified earlier this year because one of the runners "made a gesture thanking God" once he had crossed the finish line.

#13 Earlier this year, a Florida Atlantic University student that refused to stomp on the name of Jesus was banned from class.

#14 A student at Sonoma State University was ordered to take off a cross that she was wearing because someone "could be offended."

#15 A teacher in New Jersey was fired for giving his own Bible to a student that did not own one.

#16 Volunteer chaplains for the Charlotte-Mecklenburg Police Department have been banned from using the name of Jesus on government property.

#17 According to a new Army manual, U.S. soldiers will now be instructed to avoid "any criticism of pedophilia" and to avoid criticizing "anything related to Islam". The following is from a Judicial Watch article...

The draft leaked to the newspaper offers a list of "taboo conversation topics" that soldiers should avoid, including "making derogatory comments about the Taliban," "advocating women's rights," "any criticism of pedophilia," "directing any criticism towards Afghans," "mentioning homosexuality and homosexual conduct" or "anything related to Islam."

#18 The Obama administration has banned all U.S. government agencies from producing any training materials that link Islam with terrorism. In fact, the FBI has gone back and purged references to Islam and terrorism from hundreds of old documents.

#19 According to the Equal Employment Opportunity Commission, it is illegal for employers to discriminate against criminals because it has a "disproportionate" impact on minorities."

(This is the end of the segment from the Michael Snyder article.)

But let me add **#20**. Just this month some members of student government at the University of California at Irvine tried to get the American Flag banned from the campus since it symbolizes to them racism and colonialism. That hair brained piece of idiocy was vetoed but not before a number of students and professors signed a petition to get the flag banned from the campus.

(AUTHOR'S NOTE: While I mentioned in the preface that I am highly skeptical about what I read on the Internet I have seen most of the above examples covered in other venues.)

++

The following article is by Ashley Pratte, the spokeswoman for the Young America's Foundation.

The modern college campus is chock full of political correctness that fears nothing more than free speech and dissenting ideas, as 2014 proved once again. Here are 11 of the worst offenders:

1. UCSB Feminist Studies Professor Attacks Pro-Life Student.

In March, a feminist studies professor at University of California, Santa Barbara (UCSB) assaulted a 16 year-old pro-life activist who was displaying literature on campus. The professor, Mireille Miller-Young, called the pro-life group members "terrorists" after she stole their poster displaying abortion images and then proceeded to assault one of the student activists.

2. Virginia Tech Young Americans for Freedom Loses Funding Because of their Conservative Values

In the wake of a standing-room-only event with conservative activist Bay Buchanan on the topic of immigration, the VT YAF Chapter was informed that they wouldn't be receiving funding for the next two semesters. Apparently, the discussion on immigration with the former Treasurer of the United States, Bay Buchanan, irked some liberal administrators at Virginia

Tech. The Student Budget Board unanimously voted to defund the club because the event "violated the principles of community."

3. University of Michigan Requires "Race & Ethnicity" Course in Order to Graduate

In 2014 it was discovered that in order to graduate from the University of Michigan, a student must first take a course to learn how racist and intolerant the United States is toward minorities and different ethnicities. The page on the website that describes the requirement states: "all courses satisfying the requirement must provide discussion concerning: the meaning of race, ethnicity, and racism; racial and ethnic intolerance and resulting inequality as it occurs in the United States or elsewhere; and comparisons of discrimination based on race, ethnicity, social class, or gender."

4. Penn State YAF Asked to Stop Handing out Constitutions on Constitution Day

Penn State Young Americans for Freedom (YAF) activists were tabling for their organization in celebration of Constitution Day–in a designated free speech zone. After an hour or so of tabling, the YAF activists were approached by campus security personnel who told them to remove their table. The reasoning was that the students couldn't pass out flyers–even if in a "free speech" zone.

5. Blood Bucket Challenge: Anti-Semitism on Ohio University Campus

In September, the Ohio University student senate president took it upon herself to change the ice-bucket challenge. Instead, she issued a "blood bucket" challenge calling upon Ohio University to divest from Israel. She posted a video of herself wearing a bright pink shirt with the words "divest from Israel" and poured a "blood-like" substance over her head. She said the video was meant to raise awareness of the Palestinians being killed by Israel.

6. University Responses to Ferguson Protests

As a result of the Ferguson decision, we have seen numerous campuses involve themselves in protests and demonstrations. For example, Penn State held two days of "die-ins" with the President of the University posing with students with his hands up. At Smith College, the college president was harshly criticized for stating that "all lives matter." Then, Harvard Law, Columbia Law, and Georgetown Law students decided to petition for their final exams to be delayed because they were too busy protesting the decision to have time to study.

7. George Washington University Pro-Life Display Vandalized

In April, the George Washington University YAF Chapter was the victim of liberal intolerance. The YAF Chapter places crosses into the grass on the mid-campus quad in memory of the lives lost due to abortion. The students reserved space for the day and had proper permission from the university. Early in the morning, someone vandalized their sign that read, "In memory of the lives lost each year by abortion" to make it read, "In memory of the lives saved each year by abortion." By noon, the signs and crosses had been strewn into various trashcans.

8. Condom Olympics at University of Virginia

This March, the University of Virginia hosted its first annual "Condom Olympics," a "festival" of "free food, free games, free prizes, free condoms, free lube, and free online coupons" that guaranteed "information about proper condom use, safe and effective forms of birth control, STI testing, screening, and prevention, sex facts and trivia."

9. Scripps College Revokes George Will's Speaking Invitation

Scripps College created a speaker series program designed to promote conservative opinion on campus–but Pulitzer-prize winning columnist George Will was uninvited from his speaking engagement solely because of his conservative values. Ironic, huh?

10. Denver Students Protest a "Conservative" Curriculum

In September, hundreds of high school students in the Denver area stormed out of their classrooms in protest of a proposed curriculum change from the school board that would teach history in a way that promotes citizenship and patriotism. Students were under the belief that somehow American history would be "censored" if this new curriculum were taught.

11. Rutgers Faculty Protest University's Invitation to Condoleezza Rice

The Rutgers Board of Governors unanimously invited Condoleezza Rice to be the 2014 commencement speaker. Well, critics at Rutgers believe that Dr. Rice being a conservative and former member of the George W. Bush administration effectively disqualified her from addressing the commencement ceremony. According to the faculty council resolution, which passed in opposition to Dr. Rice's invitation, "A Commencement speaker… should embody moral authority and exemplary citizenship." Apparently, Dr. Rice failed on both of these accounts and was said to bring "no positive merit."

(End of article)

(AUTHOR'S NOTE: The following article by Thomas Sowell may be the most extreme example of Political Correctness in "higher" education.)

Micro-totalitarianism
Thomas Sowell

The political left has come up with a new buzzword: "micro-aggression." Professors at the University of California at Berkeley have been officially warned against saying such things as "America is the land of opportunity." Why? Because this is considered to be an act of "micro-aggression" against minorities and women. Supposedly it shows that you don't take their grievances seriously and are therefore guilty of being aggressive toward them, even if only on a micro scale.

You might think that this is just another crazy idea from Berkeley. But the same concept appears in a report from the flagship campus of the University of Illinois at Urbana. If you just sit in a room where all the people are white, you are considered to be guilty of "micro-aggression" against people who are not white, who will supposedly feel uncomfortable when they enter such a room.

At UCLA, a professor who changed the capitalization of the word "indigenous" to lower case in a student's dissertation was accused of "micro-aggression," apparently because he preferred to follow the University of Chicago Manual of Style, rather than the student's attempt to enhance the importance of being indigenous.

When a group of UCLA law students came to class wearing T-shirts with a picture of one of their professors who had organized an intramural softball game, those T-shirts were protested as a manifestation of "white privilege."
Why? Because that professor had written a book critical of affirmative action.

"Micro-aggression" protests have spread to campuses from coast to coast — that is, from California's Berkeley and UCLA to Harvard and Fordham on the east coast, and including Oberlin and Illinois in the Midwest.

Academic administrators have all too often taken the well-worn path of least resistance, by regarding the most trivial, or even silly, claims of victimhood with great seriousness, even when that involved undermining faculty members held in high esteem by most of their students and by their professional colleagues on campus and beyond.

The concept of "micro-aggression" is just one of many tactics used to stifle differences of opinion by declaring some opinions to be "hate speech," instead of debating those differences in a marketplace of ideas. To accuse people of aggression for not marching in lockstep with political correctness is to set the stage for justifying real aggression against them.

This tactic reaches far beyond academia and far beyond the United States. France's Jean-Paul Sartre has been credited — if that is the word — with calling social conditions he didn't like "violence," as a prelude to justifying real violence as a response to those conditions. Sartre's American imitators have used the same verbal tactic to justify ghetto riots.

Word games are just one of the ways of silencing politically incorrect ideas, instead of debating them. Demands that various conservative organizations be forced to reveal the names of their donors are another way of silencing ideas by intimidating people who facilitate the spread of those ideas. Whatever the rationale for wanting those names, the implicit threat is retaliation.

This same tactic was used, decades ago, by Southern segregationists who tried to force black civil rights organizations to reveal the names of their donors, in a situation where retaliation might have included violence as well as economic losses.

In a sense, the political left's attempts to silence ideas they cannot, or will not, debate are a confession of intellectual bankruptcy. But this is just one of the left's ever-increasing restrictions on other people's freedom to live their lives as they see fit, rather than as their betters tell them.

Current attempts by the Obama administration to force low-income housing to be built in middle class and upscale communities are on a par with forcing people to buy the kind of health insurance the government wants them to buy — Obama Care — rather than leaving them free to buy whatever suits their own situation and preferences.

The left is not necessarily aiming at totalitarianism. But their know-it-all mindset leads repeatedly and pervasively in that direction, even if by small steps, each of which might be called "micro-totalitarianism."

(End of article)

(AUTHOR'S NOTE: So much for the idea that universities are bastions of tolerance and the free exchange of ideas. "Fascist re-education centers" would be more appropriate. In chapter 11 we will discuss indoctrination in higher education.)

++

The following classic appeared in an article in National Review by Katherine Temf on May 5, 2015.

"Students at Arizona State University are petitioning to have the school change the 'Walk Only' signs on the school's pedestrian paths because they 'marginalize disabled bodies that cannot walk. This petition is in effort to make a more blanket title for these zones that encompasses the diversity of all bodies who occupy the community that is ASU,' states the petition, written by Alec Melger."

In other articles Ms Tempf tells of an Australian farmer who was hauled before the Royal Commission for the Prevention of Cruelty to Animals for using foul language in front of sheep. The sheep could have been offended. She also reports that PETA is demanding that the oldest bar in Britain change its name from "Ye olde Fighting Cocks" since that is offensive to chickens.

The last two examples are reasons why the term *pet owner* has been deleted from the PC lexicon and replaced with *animal guardian* since pet owner is synonymous with animal enslavement.

Ex-convict is out being replaced with "returning citizen." The Mayor of Philadelphia has mandated this term for city government usage.

Political Correctness is not about compassion and caring for the groups we listed at the beginning g of this chapter. It is really about control -- control of speech and thought. It is a tool but not an original creation of of Secular Progressivism. Political Correctness was a tool of Communism and Nazism to control speech and thought to prevent and crush opposing views. The goal of Secular Progressivism is a one Party State and if it ever comes to full power it will be just as dictatorial and tyrannical as any other dictatorship. All totalitarian regimes feel the need to stamp out freedom of expression. Communism and Nazism were able to do it through law since they came to power as full-fledged dictatorships and did not achieve power incrementally as Secular Progressivism is currently attempting in the West. Secular Progressivism has utilized Political Correctness as an effective tool to brainwash and intimidate the citizenry into fear, compliance, and acceptance. Political Correctness is driving the philosophy of Secular Progressivism into the cultural psyche as it permeates every aspect of our thought and speech causing an increasing number of people to buy into it almost by osmosis. In Europe and Canada you can be arrested or hauled before "Human Rights Tribunals" for violations of Political Correctness as we shall see in chapter 7 but it can have irreversible repercussions here in America in the workplace and in higher education. Some universities have PC kangaroo courts. It is slowly destroying freedom of speech in this country and is de facto repealing the First Amendment.

The arbiters of what constitutes Politically Correct speech and activities are the media, the universities, the entertainment industry and the government. They decide what is permissible and not permissible to do and say in contemporary culture.

I recommend three books on this topic: *Muzzled: The assault on honest debate* by Juan Williams; *The Silencing: How the Left is killing free speech* by Kirsten Powers, and *End of Discussion: How the Left's outrage industry shuts down debate, manipulates voters, and makes America less free (and fun)* by Mary Katharine Ham. Mary Katharine Ham mentions in her title that America is less fun. Political Correctness is a form of Puritanism and Puritanism is never fun-- quite the opposite.

These are all full length books on how Secular Progressivism is destroying free speech by demonizing opponents. Juan Williams and Kirsten Powers are both Liberals but not Secular Progressives which is why I do not wish to compare honest Liberals such as Williams and Powers to Secular Progressives.

Political Correctness indicates that Secular Progressives model their belief system after Communism more so than Nazism. In the '70s and '80s Secular Progressives favored Soviet backed "Liberation" movements in Asia, Africa, and Latin America. Secular Progressives would never tolerate the Nazi swastika and their current cause celebre as of this writing is removing any trace of the Confederate flag. Retail chains, Amazon, E-Bay and any other outlet that ever offered the Confederate flag for sale are falling in line and pulling it from their inventory. Secular Progressives have succeeded in getting reruns of the 1980s sitcom, *The Dukes of Hazard* taken off the air since their car sported a Confederate flag on the roof; however, Secular Progressives have no problem with Che Guevara t-shirts. Che Guevara was an associate of Fidel Castro, another Secular Progressive icon. Guevara murdered thousands of people but it is acceptable to wear t-shirts with his picture since he is politically correct being a Communist. The Secular Progressives are suckers for Guevara and other Communist figures since they purported to represent the same "victims" that Secular Progressivism purports to represent. Killing people -- well, that's just collateral damage in the service of the poor and the downtrodden. Hitler t-shirts, however, would put a Secular Progressive into cardiac arrest. Stalin is out of fashion, although he was the darling of Secular Progressives up through the 1950s when

Khrushchev exposed him for what he really was. Lincoln Steffens made his famous "I have seen the future and it works" quote about the Soviet Union in 1919, which showed that Secular Progressives loved the Leninist-Stalinist model from the beginning. Today's Secular Progressives prefer jungle guerrillas -- more sex appeal, probably; and, of course, they are "people of color."

Political Correctness is Leftwing Puritanism. It is every bit as doctrinaire as any religion. Political Correctness is filling in the moral vacuum created by the decline of traditional religion. A culture craves some kind of moral code and Political Correctness is now that moral code. It has turned Orwellian Newspeak into reality in both the United States and Europe. We may be closer to dictatorship than we realize -- a Secular Progressive Puritan dictatorship every bit as tyrannical as Oliver Cromwell's religious Puritan dictatorship in mid-17th century England.

Chapter 7

Multiculturalism

Political Correctness has incarnated itself in the cultural realm through *Multiculturalism.* Multiculturalism, per se, is not a bad thing. The United States is made up of immigrants from many cultures (E Pluribus Unum -- out of many, one). When I worked in Saudi Arabia and the United Arab Emirates (UAE), there were expatriate workers from scores of different countries and I was introduced to many different cultures. But in Saudi Arabia and the UAE there was always one *Prevalent Culture* and all other cultures were secondary and had to respect the customs and traditions of the Prevalent Culture. In Saudi Arabia that meant that Islam was the only authorized religion and all other religious services were prohibited except in embassies and private residences. In the UAE other religions could build churches (We had a cathedral in Abu Dhabi with a resident bishop) but Islam was the State Religion and other religions were forbidden from proselytizing.

(AUTHOR'S NOTE: The *Prevalent* Culture is the culture that defines the society. It does not imply superiority to other cultures; rather, it is the culture that meets our definition of culture: "Whatever works for a given people in a given place at a given time." Without a Prevalent Culture a society has no definition.)

The problem with Multiculturalism in Europe and North America is that it exists in opposition to the Prevalent Culture; not only that, it demonizes the Prevalent Culture as oppressive, xenophobic, bigoted, homophobic, racist, sexist, and generally evil and outdated. I included homophobic and sexist because Multiculturalism also encompasses gender and sexual "minorities" (Gays, Lesbians, bi-sexuals and transsexuals) -- in other words, anyone the Secular Progressive elites and government establishments deem as "victims," past and present.

In Europe it has gotten to the point where it is at least a civil, and in some cases, a criminal offense to offend a minority. 1950s sex kitten, Brigitte Bardot has been fined on five separate occasions for writing articles expressing politically incorrect opinions complaining about France being overwhelmed by Muslim immigrants and how they are changing France by refusing to assimilate and adapt to French culture and customs. On the Isle of Wight, a comedian named Simon Leger was singing a famous 1970s era hit song *Kung Fu Fighting* in a pub. Two Chinese passers-by -- not even customers of the pub but just walking by -- took offense and complained to the local police who arrested Leger for "Racism." You can burn Bibles all day long but you face arrest if you burn a Koran in some parts of Europe.

In certain European countries there are "No Go" zones where the police do not go (hence the term "No Go' zones) and Sharia (Islamic Law) is enforced. England has approximately 80 Sharia courts functioning around the country in predominantly Muslim areas. Most countries in Europe have this problem in varying degrees. Some people think it's a tossup between Sweden and France as to which will become the first European Islamic country. Swedish politician Mona Sahlin didn't help matters when she said that Sweden has no culture while Muslims have real culture -- that Sweden only has Midsummers Eve and "corny stuff like that." Sweden's constitution now obliges Multiculturalism. In Britain, Scotland Yard has a unit called The Community Service Agency dedicated to investigating anything that hints of Islamophobia, homophobia or any other real or imagined offense against "Protected Groups." Canadian provinces have Human Rights Tribunals and the British Columbia Human Rights Tribunal put pundit Mark Steyn "on trial" in absentia for allegations of racism, flying in "experts" from Philadelphia and Toronto to analyze the tone of his jokes.

The following are some more examples of this insanity posted on the *Freedom Site Blog*, April 22, 2011, run by Marc Lemire:

In Australia, the columnist Andrew Bolt is on trial for the crime of "offending" prominent members of the taxpayer-remunerated "professional Aborigine" elite. One of the complainants simultaneously "offended" a fellow Aborigine by comparing her recent appearance on TV unfavorably to an act of equine bestiality, but that's not actionable because no formally designated white people were involved — which was kind of Bolt's point in the first place: Collective rights based on race, sex, orientation, and ideology (ie, religion) destroy the concept of equality before the law.

In Denmark, despite an earlier acquittal, Lars Hedegaard of the Danish Free Press Society is to be re-tried by the State for the crime of "offending" Muslims by discussing Islam's treatment of women in a private conversation.

And in Canada the British Columbia "Human Rights" Tribunal has just fined a stand-up comic, Guy Earle, $15,000 for the crime of "offending" lesbians at a comedy club. They were drunk and were heckling him, and he unburdened himself of some putdowns. But they were homophobic putdowns, and so he must be punished. Earle was working for a fifty-buck bar tab and doesn't have 15 grand, and no comedy club in Vancouver will hire him ever again. He donated money to a gay charity in atonement, but his fellow liberals abandoned him anyway.

In all the above cases, the traditional protections of Common Law **(AUTHOR'S NOTE: Not to mention Common Sense)** do not apply -- whether the notion that truth is a defense or the principle of equality before the law. For the crime of giving offense is in the eye of the offended. A "multicultural" society needs not sensitivity training but insensitivity training — that's to say, thicker skins. The alternative is what is happening in some of the oldest free societies on earth: a state ever more comfortable in regulating the citizenry's speech, thoughts, and jokes. There's a word for that, and it isn't "diversity".

(End of Freedom Site Blog article)

The following article reflects how Stalinist Western Eyurope has become.

"A Black Day for Austria"
by Soeren Kern
December 26, 2011

An Austrian appellate court has upheld the conviction of Elisabeth Sabaditsch-Wolff, a Viennese housewife and anti-Jihad activist, for "denigrating religious beliefs" after giving a series of seminars about the dangers of radical Islam.

The December 20 ruling shows that while Judaism and Christianity can be disparaged with impunity in postmodern multicultural Austria, speaking the truth about Islam is subject to swift and hefty legal penalties.

Although the case has major implications for freedom of speech in Austria, as well as in Europe as a whole, it has received virtually no press coverage in the American mainstream media.

Sabaditsch-Wolff's Kafkaesque legal problems began in November 2009, when she presented a three-part seminar about Islam to the Freedom Education Institute, a political academy linked to the Austrian Freedom Party.

A glossy socialist weekly magazine, *NEWS* -- all in capital letters -- planted a journalist in the audience to secretly record the first two lectures. Lawyers for the leftwing publication then handed the transcripts over to the Viennese public prosecutor's office as evidence of hate speech against Islam, according to Section 283 of the Austrian Criminal Code (Strafgesetzbuch, StGB). Formal charges against Sabaditsch-Wolff were filed in September 2010; and her bench trial, presided on by one multicultural judge and no jury, began November 23, 2010.

On the first day of the trial, however, it quickly became clear that the case against Sabaditsch-Wolff was not as air-tight as prosecutors had made it out to be. The judge in the case, Bettina Neubauer, pointed out, for example, that only 30 minutes of the first seminar had actually been recorded.

Neubauer also noted that some of the statements attributed to Sabaditsch-Wolff were offhand comments made during breaks and not a formal part of the seminar. Moreover, only a few people heard these comments, not 30 or more -- the criterion under Austrian law for a statement being "public." In any event, Sabaditsch-Wolff says her comments were not made in a public forum because the seminars were held for a select group of people who had registered beforehand.

More importantly, many of the statements attributed to Sabaditsch-Wolff were actually quotes she made directly from the Koran and other Islamic religious texts. Fearing that the show trial would end in a mistrial, the judge abruptly suspended hearings until January 18, 2011, ostensibly to give him time to review the tape recordings, but also to give the prosecution more time to shore up its case.

On January 18, after realizing that the original charge would not hold up, the judge -- not the prosecutor -- informed Sabaditsch-Wolff that in addition to the initial charge of hate speech, she was now being charged with "denigrating religious symbols of a recognized religious group." Sabaditsch-Wolff's lawyer immediately demanded that the trial be postponed so that the defense could prepare a new strategy.

When the trial resumed on February 15, 2011, Sabaditsch-Wolff was exonerated of the first charge of "incitement" because the court found that here statements were not made in a "provocative" manner.

But Sabaditsch-Wolff was convicted of the second charge against her, namely "denigration of religious beliefs of a legally recognized religion," according to Section 188 of the Austrian Criminal Code.

The judge ruled that Sabaditsch-Wolff committed a crime by stating in her seminars about Islam that the Islamic prophet Mohammed was a pedophile (Sabaditsch-Wolff's actual words were "Mohammed had a thing for little girls.")

The judge rationalized that Mohammed's sexual contact with nine-year-old Aisha could not be considered pedophilia because Mohammed continued his marriage to Aisha until his death. According to this line of thinking, Mohammed had no exclusive desire for underage girls; he was also attracted to older females because Aisha was 18 years old when Mohammed died.

The judge ordered Sabaditsch-Wolff to pay a fine of €480 ($625) or an alternative sentence of 60 days in prison. Moreover, she was required to pay the costs of the trial. Although at first glance the fine may appear trivial -- the fine was reduced to 120 "day rates" of €4 each because Sabaditsch-Wolff is a housewife with no income -- the actual fine would have been far higher if she had had income.

Sabaditsch-Wolff appealed the conviction to the Provincial Appellate Court (Oberlandesgericht Wien) in Vienna, but that appeal was rejected on December 20. The court says she will go to prison if the fine is not paid within the next six months. She says she will take the case to the Strasbourg-based European Court for Human Rights.

After the trial, Sabaditsch-Wolff said her conviction represented "a black day for Austria." The Vienna Federation of Academics (Wiener Akademikerbund) said the ruling represented "politically and sentimentally motivated justice" and marked "the end of freedom of expression in Austria."

Sabaditsch-Wolff is not the only Austrian to run afoul of the country's anti-free speech laws. In January 2009, Susanne Winter, an Austrian politician and Member of Parliament, was convicted for the "crime" of saying that "in today's system" Mohammed would be considered a "child molester," referring to his marriage to Aisha. Winter was also convicted of "incitement" for saying that Austria faces an "Islamic immigration tsunami." Winter was ordered to pay a fine of €24,000 ($31,000), and received a suspended three-month prison sentence.

(End of article)

In another celebrated trial, Dutch Member of Parliament, Geert Wilders, was acquitted of "Hate Speech" for attacking the militancy of Islam and the threat it poses to modern Europe. This included unfavorable remarks about Mohammed, the 7th century founder of Islam. Wilders has been battling the European Multicultural leviathan for years. He was banned from entering Britain in 2009 due to his "extremist" views by then British Home Secretary, Jacqui Smith. This ban was overturned by Britain's Asylum and Immigration Tribunal. In 2010, Margareta Ritter, Mayor of the German resort town of Monschau, was afraid his presence would "taint" her town. In October 2012, Australia refused him a visa but that decision was overturned by Australian Immigration Minister Chris Bowen who, at the same time, attacked Wilders' "extremist" views. Wilders pushed back his visit to Australia until February 12013 but I can find no information as to whether or not he finally made it.

Australian Muslim cleric, Feiz Mohammad, called for Wilders' beheading but there is no record of the Australian government criticizing that extremism. We must keep in mind that part of this insanity is driven by fear. Radical Muslims tend to kill people and blow things up when they "take offense" so these crazy legal gymnastics are designed to head that off. We need to look at Europe since Europeans often arrive at cultural choke points before we do.

In the United States Multiculturalism includes Blacks, Hispanics, Asians, Muslims, women, Gays, Lesbians,, bi-sexuals and transsexuals. These groups are included in Europe's Protected Groups but the Muslims overwhelm all other groups in sheer numbers. Christians, Jews and White males enjoy no cultural protection since they are part of the oppressive Prevalent Culture that is saturated with racism, xenophobia, misogyny and homophobia.

The goal of Multiculturalism is the total discarding and replacement of the evil antiquated Prevalent Culture. Here in the United States, the First Amendment prevents a lot of the insanity in Europe, Australia and Canada as outlined above but we do have a form of criminal prosecution called Hate Crime Legislation. If a person of one race (or sexual preference) commits a crime against another and it appears that the crime was motivated by race or sexual preference, the perpetrator can also be charged with a "Hate Crime" that carries additional penalties. This is, in reality, double jeopardy and, therefore, unconstitutional since the Constitution prohibits being charged with the same crime twice but to get around this pesky little detail the System created an artificial crime. In fairness, people of all races and sexual persuasions have been charged with Hate Crimes but they were created with Whites in mind. It was a knee jerk Secular Progressive idea that came with the unintended consequence of having non-Whites and Gays occasionally charged with Hate Crimes. But there have been cases in diverse (no pun intended) places like Tacoma, Washington, Virginia Beach, Virginia and Baltimore, Maryland where mobs of Black youths attacked Whites and were not charged with Hate Crimes. They, or at least some of them, were charged with criminal assault but not a Hate Crime. This may be due to the theory held by some Secular Progressives that minorities are "victims" and, therefore, cannot be racist and therefore cannot hate.

American Multiculturalism, like the European variety, ridicules and demonizes the Prevalent Culture along with the traditions and values upon which that culture was built. So self-reliance, limited government and the Free Market system are attacked as concepts and institutions designed to keep minorities and women down. Traditional Judeo-Christian religious beliefs and practices are criticized as keeping women in subservience to male dominance (Ephesians 5: 22-33 without explaining the full meaning of that passage), prohibiting abortion and condemning same sex marriage both of which are constitutionally guaranteed human rights in the Multicultural New World Order.

There is an interesting dichotomy in play here. Muslims are a Protected Group in Western Multicultural societies yet Islam is outspokenly anti-Gay, anti-abortion and openly treats women as second class citizens. Being Gay merits the death penalty in Muslim countries governed by Sharia Law. But Multiculturalism views all "people of color" as victims no matter what their cultures preach and practice. Muslims qualify for Protected Group status since most of them come from lands that were once European colonies. Only Whites can be oppressors, only Whites can be racist, only Whites can be homophobic, xenophobic or misogynist. "People of color" are pristine and innocent victims of the evil White race -- regardless. And here's another interesting dichotomy: some "people of color" are actually Caucasian i.e., white -- including Hispanics and many Muslims. Consistency is not a trademark or concern of Secular Progressivism.

There is an ever growing lexicon of speech codes that can result in punitive action if used in regard to a "Protected Group." Cooking guru Paula Deen had her career destroyed for some racial remarks she had made years ago and Donald Sterling was forced to give up ownership of the Los Angeles Clippers basketball team for telling a female friend in a supposedly private conversation that she should not have had her picture taken with former basketball legend, Magic Johnson because he is Black. Trent Lott was forced to resign as Leader of the Senate Republicans for praising Senator Strom Thurmond on the occasion of his 100th birthday for his long political career which included a run for president on the Dixiecrat Party ticket in 1948. The Dixiecrats were a short-lived segregationist political party. Lott said: "When Strom Thurmond ran for president, we voted for him. We're proud of it. And if the rest of the country had followed our lead, we wouldn't have had all these problems over the years, either." This was interpreted as a direct attack on a Protected Group even if it was not intended that way. It was over lavish praise that gushed out on the spur of the moment that he should have thought through more carefully.

Numerous public figures have gotten themselves into hot water over slips of the tongue. One Washington, D.C. city official ignited a firestorm when he described the city budget as "niggardly" (as in parsimonious) which has no connection whatsoever with the "N word" the utterance of which, even in an example or quote, hangs a permanent scarlet letter around the speaker's neck. This is especially true if the offender is conservative. If he or she is liberal it somehow is not so bad. Liberal Democratic senator Robert Byrd, a former KKK member, let the "N word" slip out once and that was no problem because he belonged to the Politically Correct (Democrat) Party of Secular Progressivism which also rendered his former Klan membership irrelevant.

Speech codes get ridiculous. The term "Flip Chart" is now taboo since "Flip" was once a slang expression for Filipinos. Seattle recently banned the term "brown bag lunch" in city government communications since it may offend "people of color." When I worked for the State of Washington all State employees were required to attend Sexual Harassment seminars (a form of Sensitivity Training). The facilitator asked all the women in the class: "How many of you are afraid to use the term 'guy' in conversation?" No hands went up. Then he asked the males: "How many of you are afraid to use the word 'gal' in conversation?" Most of the hands went up. Mine did not. The women all said that the word "gal" was not offensive to them. That incident emphasized how men are intimidated in today's culture. Women, on the other hand, can call men "honey", "sweetie" and "luv" all day long.

Use of the "N" word by a non-Black can lead to all kinds of repercussions but they can call Whites "Crackers" and Honkey" and there is no problem. Jessie Jackson called New York "Hymietown", a derogatory term for Jews, during the 1988 presidential election. Contrast that to Donald Trump's remarks about criminal activity among illegal Mexican immigrants and how Mexico is pushing it's criminal element into the United States. NBC, Macy's, and Univision all broke their contracts with Trump. NBC employs the Rev. Al Sharpton who once set up a phony rape case to make Whites look bad. Louis Farrakhan uses the term "white devils." But Sharpton, Farakhan and Jackson are icons of the Secular Progressives so they can say anything they want but a conservative will be destroyed in today's Stalinist atmosphere. Secular Progressivism has effectively destroyed Free Speech in this country as well as in Europe.

It goes beyond speech codes. Brendan Eich, CEO of Mozilla, was forced to resign when it came out that he had donated $1000.00 to Proposition 8, the California initiative against same sex marriage. He made no anti-Gay slurs -- he simply donated money to a legal political cause which is a Constitutional right that every American is *supposed to* (operative term) enjoy.

So how does a group qualify for Protected Group status in the Multicultural society? The group needs to be a Certified Victim of discrimination somewhere in the history of the Prevalent Culture. It is an undisputable fact that Blacks, Hispanics, Asians, Gays and women have all been unfairly treated in American history. Never mind that the Prevalent Cultures, both here (and in Europe), took steps on their own accord to correct these wrongs. The Multiculturalist elite does not believe in moving on -- it believes in, and will enforce, unending atonement and retribution. There are no statute of limitations or sunset clauses.

It's interesting to note that Jews missed the Multicultural boat. They were barred from various clubs and organizations and were viewed with disapproval by the Prevalent Culture here in the United States well into the 1950s. They were one step above Blacks. They were a little harder to discriminate against by appearance because they were White. They were more than discriminated against in Europe. Nazi Germany systematically attempted to exterminate Jews during World War II killing millions of them in concentration camps.

In 1939 the United States refused to allow the SS St. Louis, a ship carrying 937 escaping German Jews, permission to land here even after some of the passengers on the St. Louis sent a cable directly to President Roosevelt. Only 278 would survive the Holocaust. Some were able to find refuge in other European countries but when Germany conquered those countries these people were arrested and deported to concentration camps. In fairness, the United States was not the only country that denied Jewish refugees asylum. Cuba would not allow the SS St. Louis refugees asylum nor would European countries with close diplomatic relations to Nazi Germany take in fleeing German Jews. (It's a mystery why so many Secular Progressives in the United States are Jews.)

Anti-Jewish sentiment is based in residualing anti-Semitism that has been a part of Western culture for many centuries; also, Jews are White -- not "people of color." These two factors-- anti-Semitism and white skin, plus the fact that many Jews are wealthy and successful through their own initiative -- supersede and preclude the genuine Victim Status that Jews should enjoy. As we become increasingly mired down in Multiculturalism in both the United States and Europe, we are seeing an increase in anti-Semitism and it is manifesting itself in more open hostility to Israel. Last summer (2014) the Palestinians fired over 4000 rockets into Israel from

Gaza. Israel retaliated while taking great pains to minimize civilian casualties. The world demanded that Israel -- not the Palestinians -- show restraint. Israel has become the new South Africa with increasing demands in Europe and the United States for companies and governments to divest their holdings in Israel. Multiculturalism regards Israel as a White colonial power "occupying" lands that belong to the indigenous people, the "victim" Palestinians.

Another problem for the Multiculturalists here in America is that we were founded on *Judeo*-Christian principles and Christianity is viewed as an oppressor for enforcing these principles on "victim" groups throughout our history. Jews share in that guilt as well. While anti-Semitism ebbs and flows throughout history, its present rise in the culture is a direct result of the fanatical pro-Islamic sentiment among Western Secular Progressives.

Roman Catholics should be able to claim Certified Victim status in this country thanks to a long history of discrimination that often became violent such as the burning of the Ursuline Convent in Charlestown, Massachusetts in August 1834 during an anti-Catholic riot. The American Party, also known as the Know Nothing Party, was founded in 1849 and anti-Catholicism was one of its clearly stated principles. It lasted until 1860. Anti-Catholicism was rampant well into the 20th century. Anti-Catholic radio programs were all over the dial in the 1930s and the Ku Klux Klan persecuted Catholics as vigorously as Blacks and Jews.

Anti-Catholicism was still on the American landscape when John F. Kennedy ran for president in 1960. Until then, it was a foregone conclusion that a Roman Catholic could not be elected president of the United States. The only other time a Catholic had run for president was the 1928 election where Catholic Al Smith lost to Herbert Hoover, largely because he (Smith) was Roman Catholic. Being Catholic had been widely considered as un-American since the Protestant majority believed the Catholic's first allegiance was to the Pope. John Kennedy had to answer that fear directly when he was running for president in 1960. Kennedy was emphatic at a meeting with Protestant ministers in Houston, Texas on September 12, 1960 that he would not allow any ecclesiastical interference in the discharge of his presidential duties; also, many American Protestants had crazy religious beliefs such as the Pope being the Antichrist while Catholicism was frequently referred to as "The Whore of Babylon."

Anti-Catholicism is still strong among the American elite --the media, the universities and the entertainment industry -- because of the Church's opposition to abortion, same sex marriage and physician assisted suicide -- causes all near and dear to the heart of the Secular Progressive Establishment. The New York Times, the Secular Progressive Paper of Record, recently published a portrait of Pope Emeritus Benedict XVI made from stretched out condoms. It was calling attention to the Catholic Church's opposition to artificial contraception vis a vis the AIDS epidemic in Africa. The portrait will be on display in the Milwaukee Art Museum. The Times also published that infamous picture of the Virgin Mary covered with elephant manure. But the Times would not publish the pictures of Mohammed that triggered the attack on *Charlie Hebdo*, the French Satirical journal, in January 2015 because it did not want to offend its Muslim readers. Catholics need to offend the New York Tines with mass subscription cancellations. That, however, is highly unlikely.

Ironically, American Catholics are in lockstep with the Secular Progressives on many social justice issues -- particularly illegal immigration -- but their opposition to the "Big 3" disqualifies them for inclusion in Protected Group Status. Catholics tend to vote for the Democratic candidates because Secular Progressives know how to play them for Useful Idiots in the Social Justice arena. Catholics have voted Democrat since the 19th century, so being Democrat has become part of the American Catholic identity. Breaking with the Democratic Party would be like breaking out of a cult for many American Catholics.

Muslims are a Protected Group. Some public schools teach Islam despite the ban on teaching religion in public schools; of course, teaching about Islam is disguised as cultural rather than religious studies. The Government is very careful not to use the terms "Islamic" or "Muslim" in the same sentence as the word "terrorist." (See in Chapter 6.) We are told by Secular Progressives that Muslim terrorists are not real Muslims, that Islam is a religion of peace. When Major Nidal Hassan killed 13 people and wounded 31 others at Ft. Hood, TX on Nov. 5, 2009 screaming "Allalu Akbar", the Government declared it an act of workplace violence and not Islamist terrorism so as not to offend Muslims. On Sep. 24, 2014 in Moore, Oklahoma, Alton Nolen, a Muslim convert, beheaded Colleen Hufford, a co-worker. He, too, was screaming Islamic slogans; once gain -- workplace violence. But if someone attacks an abortion clinic, the media has no trouble labeling the offender as a Christian. The Secular Progressive media tried to hang the Christian label on Timothy McVeigh who blew up the Murrah Federal building in Oklahoma City in 1995. It turned out that McVeigh was an atheist.

Secular Progressives believe that Muslims are justified in their hatred for America due to American and European exploitation of Islamic lands, and support for Israel. President Obama likes to cite the Crusades and the Inquisition as examples of Christian intolerance, so we can't be too critical of Muslims, can we? Of course, we wish they would refrain from violence but we need to understand why they are so angry.

Multiculturalism actively denigrates and degrades the traditional moral, religious and personal values that created the Prevalent Culture. In the United States that was Judeo-Christian religious values, the Free Enterprise system, limited government and self-reliance. The Protected Groups are "victims" that have been "oppressed" by these values -- slavery was often defended by Christians, never mind that the Abolitionist Movement was formed and implemented by Christians with the active support of various Christian denominations. Minorities need government protection and public assistance, something that limited government denies them. They lack the tools to be self-reliant since they have been oppressed and plundered by the Free Market system.

The Old Order has to be done away with and Judeo-Christian values and everything else that America was founded upon is now deemed evil. That includes patriotism since we are now a blend of different cultures and patriotism is equated with nationalism -- the root of the Nazi super race mentality. Nationalism bred colonialism. Multiculturalists are globalists and Multicultural societies in Europe and the United States are globalism in miniature. Globalism is the opposite of nationalism and patriotism is part of that defunct, outdated and oppressive concept.

Multiculturalism in both the United States and Europe is protected and driven by Political Correctness, speech codes, Hate Crime legislation and Affirmative Action quotas that discriminate against members of the Prevalent Culture -- White males, Jews, Christians and anyone who subscribes to traditional values. If any member of one of these Protected Groups jumps ship and professes belief in Traditional Values, they are treated with disdain a by the Cultural Elite. Conservative Blacks are called "Uncle Toms" and "House Negroes" while women are treated with disrespect in the media that would not be tolerated if used against Secular Progressive women.

In Europe, which has no First Amendment right of free speech, Political Incorrectness against Protected Groups can be civilly or criminally prosecuted. (See above.)

No society and culture can survive as divisive and destructive a phenomenon as Multiculturalism. The end result may be different in Europe than the United States. In Europe, the divide is primarily between Muslims and native born white Europeans. Within a few generations, if present trends continue, Europe will be Muslim. Muslims are gaining ground due to ongoing immigration and a higher birth rate than native Europeans. It's only a matter of time before Muslims outnumber white Europeans.

Here in the United States, we will become a nation of squabbling minorities battling for an ever diminishing package of government Entitlements. The United States will become the India of the western hemisphere within another fifty years since there will be no Prevalent Culture. We will have become thoroughly Balkanized between four main groups: Blacks, Whites, Hispanics and Asians.

Multiculturalism has its origins in four different areas:

(1) <u>Guilt</u>. Protected Groups are victims and the Prevalent Culture needs to atone for that sin and there is no statute of limitations on that atonement. Here in the United States it was slavery (Blacks), taking land away from the Mexicans (all Hispanics benefit from that) and the Indians. American Indians are a low profile Protected Group and that may be the result of their new found wealth in the gambling industry. Victims are not supposed to be prosperous and wealthy.

In Europe, it is guilt over colonialism. England and France allow people from former colonies free access to the mother country. A lot of former colonials have taken then up on their offer so they obviously enjoyed some aspects of colonialism such as order, peace and stability-- qualities that were usually lacking before the colonial powers arrived and imposed them. Once the colonial powers left, those qualities often left with them.

Scandinavia never had overseas colonies but, as Europeans, the share in the colonial guilt trip.

(2) Economics. Europe needed the taxpayers since the Continent is faced with an aging population and fewer young people to support the massive welfare systems that have come to define post-war Europe. Germany's immigrant population is the result of Guest Workers brought into the country to help with re-construction after World War II since there was a shortage of working age males in post-war Germany. The Guest Workers never left. That is part of the equation in United States Multiculturalism since foreigners, especially Hispanics, are a source of cheap labor, particularly if they are here illegally.

(3) Votes. Put Protected Groups on Welfare, accommodate their cultures, and they will vote for you. It's no secret that the Democratic Party in the United States wants as many Hispanics here as possible, legal or illegal, since the majority will vote, or eventually vote, Democrat. Hispanics who are here legally and have the right to vote will vote for the party that appears to stand up for their people and as the immigrants become citizens they will vote for that party as well.

Most of the Protected Groups in Multicultural societies have an "it takes a village" mentality and prefer Big Government. The "It takes a Village" mindset means that there is always someone there to look out for you so that you do not need to be self-reliant; in fact, self-reliance is bad since who will take care of you if you become sick, disabled or otherwise unable to work? Secular Progressivism successfully employs divide and conquer techniques pitting the Protected Groups against the Prevalent Culture.

(4) Feelings of cultural inferiority. We quoted Mona Sahlin above who openly stated that Sweden has no real culture but these immigrants have real culture. It's the old "Noble Savage" theory updated among European and American intellectuals that believe we can learn something from these non-western cultures. We see this in the attraction Eastern religions and philosophies hold for so many in the West.

114

Here in the United States, the Secular Progressive elites have come to regard the United States almost as the moral equivalent if Nazi Germany for things we did in the past to Indians, Blacks, Mexicans and various other non-western countries where we held influence. (That moral equivalency may exist regarding abortion as we noted in chapter 5.) Certainly, we did make mistakes but most of what we did was good. Show me a country that held the kind of power the United States held and accomplished better for humanity. We have made extraordinary efforts to right the wrongs we did commit, wrongs that need to be judged in the historical context of the times in which they happened. **(See Author's Note below.)** We cannot undo past mistakes but we can ensure they are corrected and will never happen again. We have done that and we continue to do that. The entire focus of Secular Progressive Multiculturalism is on the mistakes and not the good the Prevalent Culture accomplished. This holds true in both the United States and Europe.

(AUTHOR'S NOTE: "Context of the times" is an important concept. Multiculturalism judges everything, including all past historical events, in the context of today's cultural moral viewpoint. This is "Cultural Snobbery" indicating a phony attitude of moral superiority toward the past. A classic example of this is the internment of Japanese-Americans during World War II when President Roosevelt ordered all Japanese living on the West Coast to be sent to internment camps. This did not apply to Japanese living in other parts of the United States or Hawaii. In later years we, as a nation, recognized that this was wrong, formally apologized, and paid reparations to some of the survivors. At the time, however, there was a strong possibility of a Japanese attack on the West Coast. The Japanese occupied part of the Aleutian Islands and Seattle was perceived to be in danger of air raids. There were blackouts when Seattle residents were not allowed to turn on the lights after dark. So there was a real fear. In retrospect, after the war, we decided that we had been wrong but at the time it seemed the appropriate decision.)

For a society to survive it needs a Prevalent Culture with a clearly defined set of cultural values. Multiculturalism attempts to replace these traditional cultural values with an artificial set of values cobbled together from the cultural values of the Protected Groups so often at odds with, and contradicting, the Prevalent Culture. Some of the cultural practices of immigrant cultures will attach themselves over time to the Prevalent Culture through natural evolution but forcing them into the Prevalent Culture is both counterproductive and destructive since many of them run contrary to the values of the Prevalent Culture.

In Europe it is a battle between two cultures; in the United States it is a conflict between several different cultures -- White, Black, Hispanic and Asian with many variations among Hispanics and Asians since they come from different geographical areas with different cultural mores but are all lumped together under one label. In Europe, only one culture will win. In the United States none will prevail and we will become, as we said above, the India of the western hemisphere with no Prevalent Culture in a poverty stricken divided caricature of a nation.

We have drawn frequent parallels in this chapter between the United States and Europe because both Europe and the United States are following the same Secular Progressive Multicultural path. Sweden is the most Secular Progressive country in Europe. The "progress" of Sweden toward cultural suicide is well documented by British commentator, Pat Condell in his videos available for viewing on You Tube: *Ship of Fools, Sweden Goes Insane*, and *Goodbye Sweden*. I strongly recommend them.

The following article published April 9, 2015 by the Gatestone Institute International Policy Council indicates just how far things have gone in Sweden -- probably beyond the point of no return and the rest of Europe and North America (The United States and Canada) cannot be far behind.

Sweden Surrenders to Saudi Arabia

By

Ingrid Carlqvist and Lars Hedegaard

The Swedish Prime Minister stated that Sweden has no intention of ever criticizing Islam. As is customary, *Expressen* refrained from asking the PM if his comments should be taken as an indication that Sweden would stop criticizing such Islamic practices as torturing bloggers, executing infidels and oppressing women.

After weeks of diplomatic wrangling and recrimination, the Saudi government on March 27 announced that it would reinstate its ambassador, Ibrahim bin Saad bin Ibrahim al-Brahim, to Stockholm. The ambassador had been recalled on March 11 as a protest against Swedish Foreign Minister Margot Wallström's criticism of Saudi Arabia's legal practices and treatment of women. In February, she had described conditions in the desert kingdom as "medieval".

The recall of the ambassador came a day after the Swedish government announced that it would discontinue its weapons exports to Saudi Arabia.

The Arab reaction to what they saw as a deliberate denigration of Saudi Arabia and Islam was fury. In a statement, the foreign ministers of The Arab League said: "Arab countries totally reject Wallström's statement as irresponsible and unacceptable. ... Saudi Arabia's Constitution is based on the Shariah that protects the right of people and safeguards their blood, wealth and honor."

Similarly, on March 9, the Saudi cabinet, chaired by the Custodian of the Two Holy Mosques, King Salman, rejected any denunciation of the Saudi judiciary, whose decisions, it noted, are based on Islamic law and "implemented impartially to maintain the country's stability and security."

A possible deal

- Saudi Arabia is free to say that Sweden has apologized and Sweden is free to say that it has not.
- Sweden may continue to claim that it is a champion of human rights in general, but promises to tone down its criticism of abuses in Islamic countries.
- Sweden will never again criticize sharia practices and never associate such practices with Islam.
- Sweden may even have agreed to further the cause of Islam back home by, for example, promising to build new mega-mosques and giving greater influence to local imams and representatives of Islamic missionary establishments.

If the latter concession has in fact been made, it will not be hard for the Swedish government to implement it. The Minister for Culture and Democracy, Alice Bah Kuhnke, has already promised to initiate a "national strategy against Islamophobia." In Sweden, "Islamophobia" is interpreted as any criticism of Islam and mass immigration.

If the Swedish-Saudi deal is as conjectured, Saudi Arabia will have obtained de facto veto power over parts of Sweden's foreign policy -- and perhaps its domestic policies.

However one interprets the outcome of the recent diplomatic row, Sweden has suffered an immense loss of credibility. From now on, it will be hard to take seriously Sweden's claims to be a humanitarian and feminist superpower.

(End of Article and quite possibly the end of Sweden)

Chapter 8

Prejudice and Bigotry in a Culture

Along with slavery, bigotry and prejudice have been terrible blemishes on an otherwise great country. We have displayed bigotry and prejudice toward a wide variety of groups -- Blacks, Asians, Gypsies, Hispanics Homosexuals, Jews and Roman Catholics. Let's look at each of these groups since the reasons for prejudice against them vary.

Blacks

For more than a century, the cultural psyche in the south could never break free of its image of Blacks as slaves. Two centuries of legal slavery embedded this image into the southern cultural psyche and this translated into "slavery-lite" (Jim Crow laws and segregation) until the Civil Rights Movement in the 1960s. Segregation perpetuated this since it kept the two races apart and they never got to know one another. Prejudice based on race has diminished as the two races became more familiar with each other. Even in the Old South, Whites became fond and affectionate of Black servants and employees, and these included slaves in the pre-Civil War south, *because they knew them as people, as individuals* -- not just members of a strange group that lived on the other side of town. It was a similar scenario in the north since northerners (pre-1960) had very little contact and interaction with Blacks and it is human nature to be afraid of and mistrust strangers and to dislike them based on the unknown. This was often the case with foreigners immigrating to the United States with different languages and clothing styles. This was more evident with southern and eastern Europeans and their Roman Catholicism was a factor there as well. This phenomenon exists in ALL cultures and among ALL people.

Today there is a different kind of prejudice toward Blacks based on images of irresponsibility (high crime rates, high out-of-wedlock birth rates) and, recently, high profile encounters with Law Enforcement that have ended in violence and death. So-called Black "leaders" like Al Sharpton, Jesse Jackson and Louis Farrakhan blame Whites for Black problems. Farrakhan uses the term "white devils." Whites say to themselves: "We passed Civil Rights, Affirmative Action, we honor Black athletes, entertainers and others who have made a positive impact on society, given Martin Luther King a day of national recognition, elected a Black president twice and they still dislike us and can't seem to get it together in their own communities while blaming us for the problems in these communities."

Blacks, especially younger Blacks, have been programmed by their recent culture and some prominent members of the Black community to blame White people and the police for their problems. We have gone back to the 1960s in many ways in race relations. While Blacks and Whites get along in the workplace, school and other formal settings, there is a lack of informal socialization between Whites and Blacks. We feel estranged from one another due to the issues referenced above.

Problems in the Black Community have only one remedy: the restoration of the Black family, once the most solid family unit in America. The dissolution of the Black family is the root of all problems facing the American Black community. There is a distinct cultural divide between young Blacks and older Blacks. Blacks who grew up before the 1960s came from strong families that had to work together and support one another in a hostile or, at the very least, unaccepting world. Black parents transmitted clear moral values to their children, values necessary to survive in a difficult environment. They had the support of devout, faith filled Black churches. Their divorce, crime and illegitimacy rates were on a par with the Whites.

American Blacks had a unique culture that, among its other features, produced a great music tradition -- Jazz and Blues -- and great singers, the Mills Brothers and Nat King Cole among their finest. That strong culture disappeared when the Black family unit disappeared; too many young Blacks today have never known their fathers, have had no positive role models in their lives and have been programmed to distrust and dislike Whites by pseudo-leaders and vote pandering politicians (many of them White) who keep telling them that they are victims of an oppressive society and, worse, that there is nothing they can do for themselves since the deck is stacked against them. But the leaders and politicians promise more money and benefits.

Their once great musical tradition has been replaced and debased by Hip Hop and Gangsta Rap saturated with "F Bombs" and "N Bombs" that "sing" about violence against women, the police and society in general. This has had a terrible influence on young Blacks. Backwards and sideways caps and pants down to their butts convey "attitude" that appears threatening and intimidating. They hide behind Political Correctness that prohibits and proscribes any kind of criticism even, in many cases, from other Blacks who see this as a problem. All of this alienates Whites who don't want to deal with it.

The problem today is social, NOT racial. When I was working in Abu Dhabi, I was returning home late one evening and walked past a group of half a dozen or so young East African Black males. They were the only other people on the street. It was late at night but I thought nothing of it. Would my reaction have been the same if this had occurred in an American city under the same set of circumstances? Black people in the Middle East are the same as Black people in America, aren't they; racially, yes, socially, no.

Asians

Asians impressed Americans as completely foreign and different in appearance, language, culture, food, religion -- everything. Americans have always been culturally insulated being separated from the rest of the world by thousands of miles of oceans on both sides. Even today many Americans have never been outside the confines of the United States unless they have been in the military. Prejudice against Asians was based entirely on fear of the unknown. Today Asians enjoy considerable respect in the culture due to their academic and career accomplishments, solid family lives and low crime rates. We know them much better. There is more intermarriage and more socializing between Asians and Whites than there is between Whites and Blacks. (See above.) We may feel that we have more in common with Asians in terms of values.

Gypsies

Gypsies do not assimilate and inculturate and they have a reputation as petty thieves and con artists. They stay below the cultural radar screen keeping to themselves. They remain a mysterious culture both in their origins and their lack of interaction with the larger society. The majority gives them little thought but when they do come up in the conversation, it is usually negative. Gypsies are the least known and understood of American minorities. Gypsies voluntarily keep to themselves and that, together with the fact that they are such a small minority, makes it difficult to connect with them.

Hispanics

Hispanics are experiencing bad PR due to illegal immigration issues. Historically, Hispanics were looked down upon because of their accents and their "difference" but this usually disappeared after the first generation since they are Caucasian and once they lost the accent they blended in. There has been lingering resentment in the larger culture over Spanish surnamed based Affirmative Action. There is going to be a certain level of resentment as long as illegal immigration remains a problem. Gangs and a high (53 percent) out-of-wedlock birth rate cause some racial tensions as well.

Homosexuals -- Gays, Lesbians, Bi-sexuals, Transsexuals

Discrimination against Homosexuals came from the strict biblical prohibitions against homosexual activity. As religious belief declined and overall toleration of differences increased, prejudice against Homosexuals has all but disappeared from the cultural landscape. They are the one discriminated against group that has done a total cultural 180 to the point where it can now be considered cool to be Gay, Lesbian, Bi-sexual or Transsexual. The religious attitudes should have been confined to homosexual activity and not the people. Pope Francis was right when he said: "Who am I to judge."

Jews

Prejudice against Jews was based on anti-Semitism that has been around at least since the early Middle Ages. It may have originated from the early Christian image of Jews as "Deicides" followed by Jewish reluctance to assimilate together with their powerful control over financial systems. Anti-Semitism is a complex issue and it no longer has religious dimensions. The Nazis did not attempt to exterminate them based on religion, and today Secular Progressives, many of whom are atheists, are among the most virulent anti-Semites. Anti-Semitism plays a major role in the growing anti-Israel sentiment in the West. Anti-Semitism is too deeply rooted and embedded in the Western cultural psyche and it is not going to go away. It had subsided after

World war II and the Holocaust but as that recedes further into the past anti-Semitism is making a comeback.

Roman Catholics

The United States has always been a predominantly Protestant country and those Protestant beliefs were strongly held well into the 20th century. There was considerable misunderstanding of Catholics. Protestants thought Catholics put the Pope over the American government in civil authority so they viewed them as un-American. (Pope Leo XIII took the opposite view calling the American concept of Separation of Church and State the "Americanist Heresy" and that served to aggravate anti-Catholic sentiments.) That ridiculous notion of civil allegiance to the Pope wasn't totally eradicated until the election of John F. Kennedy, the first Catholic president, who made it clear during his 1960 presidential campaign that he was not going to take orders from the Pope -- as if the Pope had any intentions of taking over the country in the first place.

Today, Protestants have largely evolved away from bizarre ideas about Roman Catholicism being a satanic cult, the "The Whore of Babylon," and the Pope being the Antichrist. Fanatical Protestant preachers kept those ideas going for at least the first century and a half of the nation's existence while devout but undereducated Protestants fell for it. These preachers were on the radio well into the 1930s stirring up that insanity. Bishop Fulton J. Sheen was instrumental in turning this around with his radio and television programs from the 1930s through the 1960s. Protestants listened to him, liked him and took to heart what he was saying. Kennedy can shake hands with Bishop Sheen in Heaven and thank him for his help in getting elected.

We did not include Muslims in this discussion. Many Americans do not trust Muslims and regard them all as potential terrorists but they came on the national scene when Multiculturalism and Political Correctness were firmly entrenched so they automatically qualified for Protected Group status tight out of the gate.

The bigotry and prejudice that was sadly all too prevalent in this country for so long should not be taken as an indictment of the United States as a country since none of its foundational principles endorsed any of this. ALL people and ALL cultures are guilty of this since prejudice and bigotry have nothing to do with the nation and everything to do with human nature, fear of the unknown and lack of guidance from those who should know better. By "those who should know better" I mean the churches. Secular Progressives love to blame churches for promoting and propagating bigotry and prejudice but they never did that; what they did do was fail to proactively address these issues. That being said, the White southern Baptist and Evangelical churches succumbed to false biblical interpretations that perpetuated Black persecution in the South.

(AUTHOR'S NOTE: Southern Protestants were influenced not only by the southern cultural psyche but also by an erroneous misinterpretation of Genesis 9: 18-27. This passage somehow gave rise to the myth that Noah cursed the descendants of his son, Ham, to be "hewers of wood and drawers of water" and who received black skin as a sign of this curse. Actually, the curse was directed at Ham's son, Chanaan, whose descendants settled in what later became Israel and the curse was fulfilled when the Israelites destroyed the Chaananites. No one was "cursed" with black skin. Chapter 9 of the Book of Joshua indicates that the Chaananite Gabaonites were ordered by Joshua to be the "hewers of wood and drawers of water" for the Israelites. None of this had anything to do with Black peoples. The Chaananites were Caucasian.)

American churches should have preached against bigotry and prejudice of any kind. In a time when American churches exerted a tremendous amount of influence they could have done so much to mitigate this blight on our past. Northern churches, to their credit, preached against slavery and nurtured the Abolitionist Movement that was a catalyst in ending slavery. Toward Homosexuals they should have emphasized judgement of actions, not people.

There is still organized bigotry and prejudice in our culture but today it is directed against the Prevalent Culture and traditional values. We have already discussed this phenomenon in our coverage of Political Correctness and Multiculturalism. It is these same Secular Progressive Multiculturalists who point fingers at Christians and Traditionalist accusing them of prejudice, bigotry, and racism that are the bigots today. Secular Progressives practice the racism of low expectations by convincing minorities that they are helpless (i.e., not smart enough to rise out of poverty on their own) and that they need constant government assistance. Secular Progressives tell them that the Prevalent Culture is responsible for their cultural disintegration, not them. The

Prevalent Culture uses elf-reliance and personal accountability as a way of blaming them for things they are not responsible for -- and for which they can never be responsible.

When noted American author William Faulkner was once asked by a fledgling writer to name a good subject to write about, Faulkner replied: "Write about human nature, it never changes."

Human nature, not national philosophy, was the cause of bigotry and prejudice in this country and every other country -- not genuine and true religious beliefs, not the foundational principles of the United States; rather, human nature that is driven by fear of the unknown and the different.

Chapter 9

Our Foundational Institutions Are Disintegrating

There are five foundational institutions that support a culture and they are all crumbling away at a rapid rate. The six cultural pillars rest on these foundational institutions.

The Family

The family has been defined as the first unit of society and the American family was a cultural icon through the 1960s. Television programs such as *Ozzie and Harriet, Leave it to Beaver, Father Knows Best and Donna Reed* portrayed what may have been an idealized version, but for those of us who grew up in a traditional American family in those days, the portrayal was close to the mark. Shows like *Little House on the Prairie* and *The Waltons* focused on the American family of earlier times. All of these programs emphasized traditional American values and how they were handed down from generation to generation. The family is the first teacher of the culture.

As recently as 1960 the out-of-wedlock birth rate was 6 percent. Today (it is 40.7 percent and climbing. In the Black community it is 72 percent so it should be no shock that that demographic has the highest crime, unemployment and high school dropout rates. We have pointed out that the Black family unit used to be the strongest in American society. Secular Progressives like to blame the troubles of the Black community on poverty and racism. If that were the case why was the Black crime and out-of-wedlock birth rates comparable with the White community during the Great Depression when poverty was pandemic and racism was institutionalized, especially in the South with Jim Crow laws and segregation? Family disintegration is a major problem in all minority demographics except Asians who have the highest success rate in education and employment surpassing the White population.

Every study shows that children from fatherless homes have a much larger chance of getting involved in crime and drugs, dropping out of school and becoming permanently underemployed. It affects both genders negatively but it appears to have worse effects on young males since they lack role models to teach them how to behave like men. Single mothers cannot be fathers. Many single moms make heroic sacrifices (as my own mother did) and struggle to raise their children but they have two strikes against them right out of the gate without a responsible male figure in the house. *Responsible* is the operative word since revolving door boyfriends and the type of men so many single moms often associate with are negative and irresponsible influences. Since many of these relationships are abusive, boys grow up thinking it is normal and okay to abuse women.

We see males in today's culture in a state of prolonged adolescence. They tend to live at home well into their twenties (and in some cases beyond), fewer are going on to higher education and more of them are fathering out-of-wedlock babies and frequently abandoning the mothers since these *boys* have had no training and examples in male responsibility.

All of these factors are contributing to the de-valuation of men in modern society. Radical Feminism has been aided and abetted by irresponsible males who feed into the negative stereotypes Radical Feminism and Secular Progressivism perpetuate.

Secular Progressives blame poverty for the decline of the family. If so, why did the family hold together so well during the Great Depression? Conservatives blame easy access to Welfare and that certainly *enables* the disintegration of the family but the ultimate answer is that the moral and religious pillar of society has crumbled. The society has come to accept sexual promiscuity and applauds, literally, as we cited in the example of *the Jerry Springer Show* in chapter 5. The marriage rate is down because extramarital sex is accepted as a norm so why tie yourself down to the responsibilities of marriage? Same sex marriage dilutes marriage making it nothing special since marriage has no real definition anymore.

Another consequence of the demise of the traditional American family is the epidemic of incivility that manifests itself in road rage and all too frequent in-your-face encounters. People have been conditioned by an increasingly Secular Progressive culture to believe that they are victims and, therefore "entitled." Society tells them to stand up and fight for their rights and the government will listen; unfortunately, the rest of us have to listen too.

Had it not been for a strong family culture during the Great Depression we could have easily sunk into anarchy. Was there looting then? High crime rates? High divorce rates? Violence? None of the above; on the contrary, there was a strong sense of civil order. Today most demonstrations and acts of "civil" disobedience quickly deteriorate into rioting, violence and looting sprees. This happened recently in Baltimore when demonstrations broke out over the death of a Black man in police custody. Demonstrations quickly turned ugly and violent with plenty of looting.

A disintegrating family contributes to the decomposition of all six cultural pillars. *Politically* it creates more dependency on government Entitlements and contributes to civil disorder with higher crime rates.

It diminishes the pool of responsible, educated and drug free citizens needed to maintain a strong *military*.

It increases economic dependency on government and reduces the number of educated and skilled workers required to maintain a strong *economy*. It places an overwhelming burden on government budgets.

Large numbers of high school drop outs and a generally undereducated population greatly diminish a culture's *intellectual* tradition. Where will the scientists, engineers, teachers, musicians, composers, writers and artists come from?

The family used to instill *religious and moral* values. Religious practice has declined in direct proportion to the decline of the family. Out-of-wedlock births, extra marital sex, same sex marriage and their widespread acceptance would not happen in a culture with a strong tradition of family.

The coarsening of language (*Linguistic pillar*) is a result of the decline of the family. Let me end this section with a personal example. When I was 5 years old I picked up a string of dirty words that I used to say to my mother. She tried everything to stop me from doing that with no success until she told my father. For some reason I never said those words when he was around. Suffice it to say that after he got done with me I never said those words around mom anymore either. He permitted no further damage to the *linguistic* pillar in our house. Today bad language is "cool" and Dad's handling of my foray into foul speech would have triggered a visit from CPS.

And, as if all of the above were not enough, more than two dozen House Democrats are lining up behind a motion by Rep. Lois Capps (D, CA) that would eliminate the words husband and wife from the federal lexicon. "Those "gendered terms" would be replaced by "gender-neutral" words like "spouse" or "married couple," according to Capps. The State of Tennessee tried to replace the words *mother* and *father* with *parent number1* and *parent number 2* on official state documents but backed off hwhen the public decided that was going too far. This idiocy comes in the wake of the June 26, 2015 Supreme Court decision legalizing same sex marriage in all 50 states.

The Neighborhood

The old fashioned American neighborhood was an extension of the family. There was little transiency in and out of the neighborhood, neighbors formed bonds and the environment provided children with surrogate parents, brothers and sisters. The neighborhood was a safe haven. Small businesses -- grocery stores, hardware stores, dime stores, butcher shops, barber shops, drug stores, cafes and medical and dental offices could all be found in the immediate vicinity. The neighborhood was a cradle of American democracy since neighborhoods were the epicenter of the New England Town Hall meetings. Churches played a vital role in the old American neighborhood.

The traditional American neighborhood began its decline in the mid-1960s. Women started working in large numbers so fewer of them were home when the children came in from school. This perpetuated the "Latchkey Kid" phenomenon -- children carrying their own set of keys because nobody was home to let them in after school. This adversely affected the neighborhood bonding which was held together by housewives with their coffee klatches, visiting over the back fence and dropping in on each other during the day.

The small businesses were replaced by chain stores, box stores, strip malls and super malls located at a distance from the neighborhood. As people changed careers and the economy experienced more fluctuation, there was more movement in and out of neighborhoods. Upward mobility destroyed the ethnic neighborhoods that were a hallmark of 19th and early to mid-20th century America. Families were spending less time at home, either at work or driving children all over town to various organized activities.

The rise in child kidnappings and disappearances have driven the kids off the streets, sidewalks and vacant lots into organized activities which are ultimately artificial lacking the spontaneity and creativity of children of a few decades ago. That spontaneity and creativity have been replaced by mindless addiction to machines and social media.

The neighborhood was an extended family and other parents on the block had no problem reprimanding someone else's children. If another parent caught a kid lying, stealing or swearing it was the same as the child's own mom and dad addressing the inappropriate activity. Today we'd sue but no problem since we don't even know who lives next door much of the time. You don't see children playing outside, the corner store is gone and moms aren't chatting over the back fence after putting the clothes out on the line, No one drops in for coffee in the evening -- in fact, many of us no longer answer our doorbells, especially after dark; saddest of all, no one seems to care. These characteristics of the American neighborhood once defined *Americana*, a cultural phenomenon that is now gone. You can still see it in collections of Norman Rockwell's paintings in old issues of *The Saturday Evening Post*. The traditional American neighborhood has been replaced by *the anti-neighborhood*, the mega apartment complexes that have all the charm of old East Berlin tenement blocks.

The Workplace

The traditional American workplace has undergone massive change in the past 50 years. Much of this change has been driven by technology but it has major cultural aspects. Throughout American history until the 1960s, you could get a job straight out of high school and stay in that job with that company until you retired. This was the case with all of my family members in my grandparents' generation. My grandfather started out bicycling around Akron, Ohio rounding up railroad crews for the Baltimore & Ohio Railroad when he was 13, back before most people had telephones. 56 years later he retired as Terminal Train Master for the

Baltimore & Ohio in Akron. He accomplished all of this with only some high school education. That will not happen today.

Nine factors have come into play to change this:

(1) Technology has rendered many entry level jobs obsolete and has made others much more complex. That same job that required you to know how to use a telephone and a typewriter 50 years ago now requires knowledge of Word, Access, Excel and PowerPoint as well as one or more company computer programs -- not to mention how to program the office telephone at your desk.

(2) Higher taxes and more complex and burdensome regulations that cause many small businesses to close or just not start up. The small business used to be a bedrock employer.

(3) Foreign competition and outsourcing. These are fairly new developments but they are a major cause of job loss.

(4) The disappearance of the American industrial base that was the backbone of the middle class providing millions of well-paying jobs that required little formal education and training.

(5) The tendency to lay employees off during economic downturns. Employers now look at employees as dispensable commodities. During the Great Depression, the Kellogg Cereal Company in Battle Creek, Michigan had to cut back on hours but they did that rather than fire employees. Employers used to care about their employees and employees returned this consideration with strong loyalty. Today that mutual loyalty is gone. The Bottom Line is all that matters to most employers today.

(6) Massive influx of foreign workers. Part of this is due to the lack of technical expertise among native born workers and part of it is caused by excessive immigration both legal and illegal. A recent Department of Labor study shows jobs remaining flat for native born workers but they have increased 5 percent for foreign born workers. Again, this is due to the need for technical skills lacking among the native born and that immigrants will work for less pay -- especially illegal immigrants.

(7) Native born Americans are not acquiring the technical skills needed to compete successfully in today's marketplace.

(8) The decline of locally based businesses. Most workers today work for big corporations that may be headquartered across the country, run by bureaucrats who care only about profits. The employee is not a person -- just a number and if profits require layoffs or closing entire stores, oh, well, too bad. The sense of anomie that has penetrated the family and the neighborhood has extended into the workplace.

(9) The disappearance of pension plans replaced by 401Ks with employers that are only too willing to halt their contributions when the economy takes a dive. Some state and municipal governments are moving to 401Ks in lieu of traditional pension plans.

The Churches

The Churches -- Catholic, Protestant and Jewish -- used to be the moral anchors and beacons of American culture. You could be sure you would learn what was right and what was wrong when you went to church on Sunday. The churches were instrumental in stoking the fires of the American Revolution by pointing out the injustices of the British colonial administration. American churches actively supported the Abolitionist Movement to end slavery. Today they are bastions of Political Correctness. The mainstream Churches say little, if anything, about abortion, homosexuality, extra-marital sex and the overall coarsening of American culture.

But they are major purveyors of "Social Justice"; however, their approach to Social Justice is selective. They defend trendy causes and the rights of fashionable minorities, those minorities that are defined as "victims" by the Secular Progressive elites. Not all groups qualify. Middle Eastern Christians are being beheaded, crucified, buried alive and burned alive (only the lucky ones are shot) and Christian girls and women are routinely raped and sold into slavery by radical Islamic militants. They may receive a few prayers once in a while in church but they do not benefit from the same moral outrage these churches demonstrate when a Mexican illegal gets deported. The mainstream Churches have had a noticeable effect on social disintegration in the United States due to their silence on moral issues that should be at the top of their agendas.

The mainstream Churches -- the major Protestant denominations and a large part of the Roman Catholic Church -- have failed miserably in addressing cultural decline. They do nothing when Christian business owners are prosecuted for refusing to cater same sex weddings on religious grounds. The Affordable Health Care Act (Obamacare) is trying to force Roman Catholic religious institutions to provide contraceptive coverage in their employee health insurance policies. The Little Sisters of the Poor have been in the news recently over that issue. Roman Catholics should be hearing about this from the pulpit but they are not.

Churches roll over for the government. In 2009 President Obama delivered a speech on the economy in Gaston Hall at Georgetown University in Washington, D.C. The Administration requested that the symbol for Christ, HIS, on the stage where Obama would be speaking be covered up. The official reason was that they wanted a simple setting of flags, pipe and drape. The University complied.

Statistics on regular church attendance vary from 20-40 percent depending on which study you read. Americans are migrating away from traditional church attendance for a variety of reasons, a major one of which is that they are getting a lot of fluff and no substance. Churches expend too much energy on culturally popular causes -- Gay Rights, immigration, women clergy, and "the Poor and the marginalized." They avoid any topic dealing with cultural disintegration; so, while they were once part of the solution providing strong moral guidance and leadership, they have become part of the problem repeating and representing fashionable Politically Correct attitudes toward cultural problems or avoiding them altogether. Most clergy want to avoid controversy since that drives people -- and money-- away.

The churches seem blissfully unaware of the growing restrictions on religious liberties in this country, some of which we have already detailed in this book, and is further covered in some more detail in an article by Todd Starnes published in the Feb. 20, 2014 edition of *Townhall* posted at the end of this segment. Secular Progressives still regard Christianity as a threat even though religion appears to be losing the cultural war. Secular Progressives fear a religious renaissance and are afraid that this lack of leadership in American churches may be only temporary.

Survey: Christians Losing Culture War

By

Todd Starnes

According to a new survey from LifeWay Research seventy percent of senior pastors at Protestant churches say religious liberty is on the decline in the United States and 59 percent of Christians believe they are losing the culture war. Eleven percent considers that war already lost.

The survey results are staggering– indicating grave concerns about the moral direction of the nation from both the pulpit and the pew.

"Ten years ago we were talking about who would win the culture war and now we're talking about how will Christian rights be protected after the culture war," Ed Stetzer, the president of LifeWay Research told me. "We've lost our home field advantage. There are going to be some things that are different."

Stetzer said it's a big shift. "And it's a shift I would not have guessed," he told me.

Over the past few years, I've documented hundreds of instances of religious persecution in the United States. And the targets have been exclusively Christians. The military labeled evangelical Christians and Catholics as religious extremists. Christian organizations like Family Research Council and American Family Association were labeled by the military as domestic hate groups. Bibles were briefly banned from Walter Reed Medical Center.

The Internal Revenue Service targeted Christian ministries engaged in pro-life activities. The government demanded to know the content of one group's prayers. A Wyoming church was ordered by government officials to turn over their membership roles. A Baptist newspaper in North Carolina was audited – as was America's evangelist – Billy Graham. The list of attacks on Christians goes on and on – from students ordered to stop praying in front of the Supreme Court to chaplains being told they could no longer pray in the name of Jesus.

In recent days, the battleground has pitted gay rights groups against Christian-owned businesses who cater to the wedding industry. Christian bakers, florists and photographers have been hauled into court and brought up on state discrimination charges for declining to participate in same-sex weddings. And in every single instance – lower courts have ruled that gay rights trump religious rights.

So perhaps it should not be a surprise that 70 percent of pastors and 54 percent of Americans believe religious liberty is on the decline. Scott McConnell, vice president of LifeWay Research, said the concern is widespread. "Half of Americans say that religious liberty is on the decline," he said. "That's a lot of people."

Robert Jeffress, the pastor of First Baptist Church of Dallas, Tex., conceded that Christians are losing the culture war and they are losing ground every day. "The primary reason Christians are losing the culture wars is that pastors are AWOL when it comes to informing and energizing their congregations," Jeffress told me. "Unless Christians stand up and engage the political process," Jeffress fears there may come a day when religious liberty is extremely curtailed. "A religious leader once said, 'my successor will see the tax exempt status removed from churches and his successor will go to jail,' " Jeffress said. "That is probably on the horizon."

But there are some pockets of resistance – like the town of Greenwood in the Mississippi Delta. Jim Phillips is the senior pastor of North Greenwood Baptist Church. He told me that Greenwood still has a "very high respect for the historical Judeo-Christian ethic… Every one of my son's community college football games around the state last season began with a prayer on the loud speaker – in Jesus' name," he told me. "Will that eventually be challenged? I suspect so at some point… But right now pockets of religious boldness still exist," Phillips said national trends, though, are disturbing. "Christians have slowly given away their impact on culture by becoming worldlier instead of confronting the culture to become more and more godly," he said.

So who is to blame for the loss? Phillips blames Christians. "Sadly, Christians have often wimped out and grown silent instead of being bolder for the Gospel," he said. "Christians get subdued into thinking they're not supposed to rise up."

Jeffress agreed with that assessment and said the church must involve itself in the political process. "There are 50 to 80 million evangelicals in America," he said. "Only half are registered to vote and only half of those voted in the last election."

Jeffress said it's imperative for people of faith to engage the culture. "Every time we go to the voting booth we are casting a vote for righteousness or unrighteousness," he said.

Pastor Phillips also urged his fellow pastors to step up to the plate. "My calling is to keep leading the charge," he said. "As a local pastor, my goal is to keep encouraging my church to seek to raise the bar and not lower it when it comes to confronting culture."

Stetzer said he hopes the survey will spark a "fruitful national conversation about religious liberty concerns. The perception was that the culture war was once a winnable war but it's switched from an offensive battle to a defensive battle."

Pastor Jeffress urged Christians to stand their ground. "We ought to do everything we can to push back against this encroachment on religious liberty and protect our right to spread the Gospel. I write about this very issue in my new book, *God Less America*. It will be published in May (2014). But I'm reminded of a quote by President Ronald Reagan: 'If we ever forget that we are one nation under God, then we will be a nation gone under.' A few years ago, a New York public school teacher was ordered to remove that quote from her classroom wall. She was told that it violated the U.S. Constitution. I'm afraid we may be "gone under."

(End of article)

Secular Progressives know that they can get away with the discrimination referenced in this article for five reasons:

(1) They know Christianity is on the decline in this country and the majority of people won't care.

(2) They know there is no leadership to organize resistance and, if necessary, civil disobedience such as we saw during the Civil Rights movement in the 1960s.

(3) Some mainstream churches are in favor of same sex marriages and will perform them while others do not object to physician assisted suicide. It's easy to employ divide and conquer strategies between the liberal mainstream churches and the conservative churches. Mainstream Protestantism and Roman Catholicism are in agreement on most social justice issues. The Roman Catholics will usually put up no more than token resistance to abortion while mainstream Protestantism ignores it.

(4) The Roman Catholic Church cannot break its century and a half old bond with the Democratic Party no matter what the Party does. William F. Buckley Jr once described the Catholic Church as "The Democratic Party at prayer." Many Catholics still regard the

Republicans as the anti-Catholic country club party. This may explain why there has been so little reaction from the Catholic hierarchy to attacks on religious freedom. Most of them grew up in solid working class Democratic households.

(5) Most Christians are uninformed about the Secular Progressive campaign against religious liberty. It is analogous to the frog being boiled slowly in hot water. Before most Christians realize what is happening, it will be too late. Secular Progressivism and its agenda succeed when the majority of the electorate is uninformed.

The Schools

Schools here fall into two categories: the Public School system and Higher Education (colleges and universities).

Public School System

Conservatives often portray the public schools as teaching homosexuality, Sharia Law and what an awful country the United States has been throughout its history. You can certainly find examples of this but the real problem with the American Public School system is that it is broken. Up until the 1960s the schools operated "in loco parentis" -- in the place of the parent. This meant that they were free to discipline the students and maintain order. Schools had the full support of the parents and you could receive an excellent education in a public school. As the culture started granting everyone "rights", students were no exception. Dress codes and corporal punishment were abolished. Teachers were not allowed to yell at students or call them stupid. **(AUTHOR'S NOTE: I had a teacher in high who started almost every class with what became his mantra: "You guys are so stupid.")**

As families started breaking down, the schools were dealing with increasing numbers of dysfunctional students with serious issues and problems. As these issues increased, the authority given to teachers and administrators was correspondingly decreased. Verbal and physical assaults on teachers became routine especially in inner city schools. A local vice-principal I knew from the gym was telling some of us that a female student said: "F*** you, Dr.---." One of the guys asked him why he allowed her to say something like that: "Well, at least she called me Dr.----," he answered.

In this kind of environment teachers aren't indoctrinating, they are trying to survive and many quit before they reach the 5 year mark. Indoctrination is not effective with students up through high school, anyway. They are there because they have to be and are too absorbed in their electronic gadgets to pay attention to anything else. One of the biggest classroom management problems is keeping students off of their cell phones and machines. And while we are on the subject of indoctrination-- I'm a product of the greatest indoctrination system ever invented -- the pre-1960s Catholic grade school. It may still be studied by North Korean propaganda experts. If so, they needn't bother. Most of my grade school contemporaries no longer attend church. So what makes anyone think the public schools are going to churn out faithful Marxists?

Indoctrination is not effective despite the Political Correct approaches the schools take toward social studies. There is an emphasis on mistakes the country has made in its history such as slavery and treatment of American Indians. If it happened it should be taught and not whitewashed over but the accomplishments America has achieved need to be given full emphasis as well and too many public school curriculums are failing to do this. It is more of an issue what they are not teaching rather than what they are teaching. They are de-emphasizing History, civics and social Studies.

And there are incidents like these: In 2011 in McAllen, TX, Brenda Brindson, was flunked in one of her classes for refusing to recite the Mexican Pledge of Allegiance and sing the Mexican National Anthem. (Interestingly, Brenda's mother is a Mexican immigrant and she is fluent in Spanish.) The McAllen Independent School District has policies against compelling students to recite the American Pledge of Allegiance if the student has conscientious or religious objections. All schools have that proviso since some religious groups (Jehovah's Witnesses) have religious objections to it. Brenda filed a lawsuit; another example of Multiculturalism on steroids.

In 2010 at Live Oak High School in Morgan Hill, CA five students were sent home for wearing American flags on their T-shirts at a school Cinco de Maio celebration. School administrators told them to either turn the T-shirts inside out or go home. The school felt the display of the American flag would offend Mexican students celebrating Cinco de Maio.

These two examples are more examples of Multiculturalism run amok than ideology or indoctrination. Multiculturalism submerges the Prevalent Culture in favor of Protected Groups and Hispanics are a Protected Group. This seemed to be the case in McAllen and at Live Oak High School.

The Government further burdens schools with programs like "No Child Left Behind" which is test-centered forcing teachers to teach to standardized tests because if the students do not do well on these tests the schools will be penalized and, in some cases, closed. The schools are feeling all of this pressure. (See Chapter 5 for a major example of what this led to in the Atlanta, GA School District.) The only public schools that produce good results are those in affluent neighborhoods. Parents are looking for alternatives creating a growing demand for private and charter schools. In the New York City school district (that encompasses all five boroughs) the White student enrollment is only 15 percent.

The latest statistics claim a 7 percent high school dropout nationwide but that statistic can be misleading. Dropout rates are low in private and charter schools and public schools in affluent areas. It is well into double digits in inner city schools. The statistics do not factor in home schooling which is on the rise.

If you want to see how far we have declined, go on line and look up 8th grade tests from the 1890s and see what students had to know if they expected to walk out of the 8th grade with a diploma in hand. Snopes downplays them but there is a lot of information on them that I remember having to be familiar with in my grade school and high school days. It can also be argued that most children did not finish 8th grade much less go to high school 100 years ago but those that did, learned. Today they are not learning. Educational Testing Service in Princeton, NJ released a study that shows American students at the bottom rung of the industrialized nations in math and technology and 16th in literacy. There is an exerpt from that study at the end of this chapter.

Self-esteem is so important today but just a few decades ago it had to be earned. I'm a graduate of the Catholic school system. I graduated from Bellarmine High school (Jesuit) in Tacoma, Washington in 1964. We were assigned classrooms in our freshman year based on our entrance test scores -- there were four freshman classrooms, A, B, C, and D rooms. Guess what "D" de facto stood for. "D" Room was located directly adjacent to the back door. On our first day there the principal marched all of us newly minted freshmen (Bellarmine was all boys in those days so freshMEN is acceptable here.) into the gym and told us point blank that half of us were going to flunk out. He was right. 122 of us started and 70 graduated but that included a number of students who came on board as the years passed; so half of the original class did flunk out or leave. We were frequently told that we were stupid, knocked over the head with books and had our butts pounded up between our shoulder blades if we got out of line. In 2013, I visited Bellarmine and talked to a teacher who was in my old freshman classroom ("C" Room). I recounted some of these stories and she was appalled: "We could NEVER say and do that to these kids today." Bellarmine is now co-ed but that shouldn't make any difference. The girls were getting the same kind of treatment at the two Catholic Girls schools in Tacoma when I was at Bellarmine. Today kids get trophies for just showing up. That only adds to the Entitlement mentality.

Public schools are no longer teaching cultural literacy. Students are graduating with no solid knowledge of history and civics. They have no understanding of the cultural traditions of the United States. Cultural decline accelerates when you start piling up generations with little or no knowledge of the Prevalent Culture which is what is happening today. No surprise there since Secular Progressives control American Public Education and have established Multiculturalism as the curriculum. Yes, we lag behind the rest of the world in math, science and engineering but the total lack of cultural literacy is far worse. William Bennett wrote a book called *Cultural Literacy*. It should be a required class in every school and a requirement for graduation. Multiculturalism has a lot to do with this because it is the major driver in cultural decline since schools don't want to pass on the Prevalent Culture so as not to "offend" students who came here from other cultures. That does not indict all teachers as Marxists -- it indicts a broken public school system.

Higher Education

The American universities lead the world in medicine, science, technology and engineering. People come from all over the world to attend our universities specializing in those fields. The problem is with the Liberal Arts schools. The idea of a university is to promote and encourage the free exchange of ideas where all are welcome to expound their viewpoints and those who articulate their positions in the most knowledgeable and logical manner win the debate. Since the 1960s, many Liberal Arts schools have been taken over and dominated by Radical Leftists who teach Marxist philosophy and economics while attacking and denouncing the Free market System, label the United States as an oppressor nation and openly support regimes hostile to the United States. They adore Castro's Cuba citing its "superior" healthcare system. (How many of them go down there for treatment?) They promote radical social agendas and are avowedly anti-Christian in teaching those agendas. Conservative speakers are routinely shouted down by students, encouraged and often led by radical professors, if these conservatives somehow make it to the stage to speak. Jeanne Kirkpatrick, Henry Kissinger, Condoleeza Rice, Ann Coulter, Christina Hoff Summers, the Minutemen and various Christian groups have over the years either been shouted down or "disinvited."

Many of these universities have Orwellian speech codes that virtually prohibit freedom of speech by banning all opinions contrary to Secular Progressive dogma. Conservative students will be punished by failing grades, ostracism and sometimes hauled before kangaroo courts for violations of the University speech code. These students may be expelled or sentenced to cultural sensitivity or diversity training; in other words, sentenced to a version of a Communist re-education center.

The following are excerpts from an article titled *Campus Speech Codes: Civility or Tyranny*? By James M. Wallace

Last year at the University of Pennsylvania, a student named Eden Jacobowitz was in his room studying one night. His studies were interrupted by the shouting and stomping of a group of black sorority sisters. He and other students yelled out of their windows to get their peace and quiet back. He made a reference to "water buffalo"; many of the others used racial epithets. The sorority sisters took offense and called the campus police.

During the investigation by campus police, the sorority sisters could not identify any of the people who had yelled at them, but only Eden Jacobowitz admitted to having yelled out of his window. He naively assumed that he had done nothing wrong. He thought the sorority sisters were the ones who had done wrong. He acknowledged that he had referred to them as "water buffalo" and explained that the Yiddish word for water buffalo, when used as an insult, meant "a noisy, oafish person" much the same as the English word "cow."

The sorority sisters (who had caused the problem in the first place) filed a formal complaint with the university administration. The campus police presented the results of their investigation to the administration. Under university regulations, the administration charged Eden Jacobowitz with making racially insensitive remarks. Using his own admission acquired before he had been advised of his rights, the administration found him guilty even though it was unclear as to how the expression "water buffalo" had any racial connotation. Apparently, the fact that he was white and his "victims" were black was sufficient evidence of racist intent. He was required to attend "sensitivity training classes" but refused, still insisting that he had done nothing wrong. Presented with his willful disobedience, the administration scheduled a hearing to determine if they should expel him from the university.

At this point, the conservative press picked up the story partly due to the nomination of University of Pennsylvania president Sheldon Hackney to head the National Endowment for the Humanities. Conservative commentator Rush Limbaugh gave the story extensive play on his radio show including the reading of a letter from Eden Jacobowitz detailing his troubles. The national press then took up the story. The increasing publicity and the negative reaction to it embarrassed the university administrators into dropping the matter and clearing Eden Jacobowitz's name.

++

Like Eden Jacobowitz, numerous students and professors in universities across the country have found themselves accused of violating "speech codes" for simply making comments that were perceived as "racist" or "sexist" by members of a "protected minority class." Even a casual review of these cases reveals a startling pattern. The perpetrator of this "crime" is usually a white male (sometimes with impeccable liberal credentials), and the "victims" are "persons of color" or "persons of gender." Either white males are hopeless racists and sexists, or the people perceiving them as such are.

Particularly telling is the fact that "hate speech" from a "protected minority" member is rarely, if ever, punished. One almost never hears any condemnation of the virulent anti-Semitism of some black students or the patently sexist attitude behind the radical feminist assertion that "all men are rapists." Apparently "victims" can't be victimizers.

+++

The most dangerous threat posed by "speech codes" is the subversion of the university's mission. In a speech in New York City on March 20, 1991, Yale University President Benno C. Schmidt, Jr. sounded the warning.

"Some of the finest universities in this country have adopted rules which empower groups of faculty and students with roving commissions to punish offensive speech." When this happens, he concluded, "a lethal and utterly open-ended censorship is loosed." Its greatest damage is not to those punished, but to "the vastly greater number of speakers who will steer clear of possible punishment," and the "chilling effects of vague powers to punish offensive speech"

(End of excerpted article)

No Liberal university has stood up for Middle Eastern Christians being massacred in the ISIS orchestrated genocide but they will hit the streets for illegal immigrants facing deportation or Palestinians sending thousands of rockets into Israel.. These universities are both anti-Christian and anti-Semitic. Recently UC Davis sponsored a pro-Palestinian rally where students screamed "Allalu Akbar", the Radical Islamic battle cry. One wonders if those idiots realized that Allalu Akbar means "God is great." Probably not or they would not have said it. They went on to spray paint swastikas on a building occupied by a Jewish organization on campus.

Anti-Christian attitudes predominate on these campuses. At Florida Atlantic University in Boca Raton, FL., Professor Deandre Poole, was teaching a course on *Intercultural*

Communications and directed the students to write the name of Jesus on a piece of paper and then put it on the floor and stomp on it. When one of the students, Ryan Rotela, respectfully refused he was suspended by the university. This story hit FOX News and Conservative Talk Radio and the school backed down and apologized. Would they have done so without the publicity? Deandre Poole was active in the local Democratic Party which underscores the anti-Christian element in that Party.

Christian students are frequently challenged and put on the spot for their beliefs in American universities.

The worst example I've come across is Saida Grundy, Assistant Professor of Sociology and African-American Studies at Boston University. This woman has sent out thousands of Tweets over the years, many of them vicious racist attacks against Whites. She says that during the week of the Martin Luther King holiday she makes every effort to avoid spending any money at White owned businesses. She laments that she finds this "nearly impossible." Here arefour more examples of these toxic tweets: **(1)** "For the record NO race outside of Europeans had a system that made slavery personhood instead of a temporary condition**." (AUTHOR'S NOTE: What does *personhood* mean here?); (2)** "In other words, deal with your white s*it white people. Slavery is a Y'ALL thing."; **(3)** "Why is white America so reluctant to identify white college males as a problem population."; **(4)** "White people are all Ben Affleck. These euphemisms like "farmer" and "pioneer" means owned humans and killed natives." She blames slavery completely on Europeans conveniently leaving out the role Arabs and her fellow Black Africans played in the slave trade. The Whites did not go into the interior. They waited at the ports for others to bring slaves to them and those "others" were often other Blacks. She claims that Europeans invented generational slavery as if in other cultures, children born to slaves were not slaves. Something else she (and all other Secular Progressives) conveniently omits is the number of Blacks who owned slaves in the pre-Civil War south. If you care to look into it I recommend *Dixie's Censored Secret: Black Slave Owners* by Robert Grooms.

The problem is not just poor and erroneous scholarship which should disqualify her for a teaching position in the first place; it is the toxic racism of this woman. Could a White student take her class -- even the most liberal White student? This person obviously hates Whites and no amount of Political Correctness is going to hide that. So what was Boston University thinking of when they hired this academic quack? Didn't someone check her writings -- and her tweets? As long as Saida Grundy is on the Boston University payroll that institution cannot call itself a university with a straight face. "Racist Think Tank" is what it is now.

Perhaps as bad as Saida Grundy is Zandria Robinson, a Sociology professor at the University of Memphis who also sends out toxic tweets equating "whiteness" to terror and implying that the mass murder at a Black Charleston, South Carolina church was normal for Whites. She also tweeted that death and rape threats were expressions of love from conservative Whites. She also threatened to "come after" any White student who claimed that Blacks receive preferential treatment in acceptance to graduate school. She is no longer employed by the University of Memphis but she claims she had taken another job. She says she is not a racist and that she has "a white friend." My personal opinion is that she probably did have another job lined up because these universities will tolerate anything from a minority but would fire a White professor in a New York second for coming up with that kind of garbage.

In Stone Mountain, Georgia Nancy Gordeuk, director of a private school was fired for using the term "Black People." A ruckus developed when she called security to eject a man who was disrupting the graduation ceremony taking "selfies." The man was Black and the audience didn't like the way it was being handled and some of them got up and left prompting Gordeuk to exclaim that "all the Black people are leaving." She apologized all over the place, the local NAACP got involved and some want to pull the school's accreditation probably because Gordeuk owns the school.

At Duke University, Professor Jerry Hough is "on leave" for writing that Blacks refuse to assimilate and take "strange new names." Colleagues were outraged but Hough is not backing down. But no one says anything about Grundy and Robinson. This is blatant double standard and is destroying both education and race relations and taking the culture down with it in the process.. It's certifiably insane.

Higher Education is the new front line on the war on men. We hear a lot about the bogus non-existent "war on women" that the Republicans are accused of waging on women but there is a real war on men that is being waged on college campuses. Four cases underscore this: **(1)** The Duke University rape case in 2006 in which three members of the Duke Lacrosse team allegedly raped a Black woman hired as a stripper at a party. The local district attorney, Mike Nifong, took a "damn the torpedoes, full speed ahead" attitude wanting to charge them with both rape and a hate crime. The case fell apart, the three men were vindicated and Nifong ended up getting disbarred; **(2)** In 2012 *Rolling Stone Magazine* published an article about a freshman co-ed allegedly gang raped at a fraternity party. This story was also a fabrication but Rolling Stone ran with it but had to retract it when an independent study by the Columbia University Journalism Department debunked it; **(3)** In 2012 an Amherst male student was accused of rape and subsequently expelled even though his innocence was proven largely through text messages from his alleged victim; **(4)** In perhaps the most bizarre case, Emma Sulkowicz of Columbia University carried a mattress around with her as a form of crusade against campus sexual assault. Emma scored an invitation to attend the State of the Union Address from New York Democratic Senator Kirsten Gillibrand. In this, as in all cases, the preponderance of evidence was on the side of the accused.

In the Amherst case and possibly Columbia, the schools were acting under directives from the Obama department of Educatio0n designed to protect alleged rape victims by not demanding sufficient evidence and willingness to take the victim's word and not subject her to any kind of cross examination for fear of intimidating her. Colleges and universities are afraid of losing federal money if they don't comply so they violate the accused's Constitutional Rights, especially the right of Due Process even when there is strong evidence in the defendant's favor.

Higher Education has become a Stalinist enclave ruled by Orwellian speech codes, kangaroo courts for members of groups out of favor with Secular Progressive ideology, and banning of all opinion opposed to the Secular Progressive ideology. In most of these sexual assault allegations, the guy usually did something stupid -- not illegal -- stupid -- to trigger it. In all honesty, if I had a college age son I'd advise him against dating any co-eds and even avoid close friendships with them. That's simply where we are in 2015.

While the driver in the public schools is Multiculturalism, the driver in Higher Education is Secular Progressive ideology. Many college and university faculty are committed Secular

Progressives who deliberately set out to indoctrinate their students. That's how many of them became Leftists -- indoctrination during their own college days. Students in Higher Education are more susceptible to ideas since they are in college to expand their intellectual horizons and are open to ideas. It is easy to convince them to read Maya Angelou instead of Dead White Males since she is "relevant" and relevance is important to college students. College and university students have social consciences so they easily fall for the "America the Oppressor" indoctrination when professors give detailed accounts of slavery, blaming Christianity for perpetuating slavery in the South, or neglecting to mention the vast number of White Union soldiers who died in the Civil War that ended slavery in America. These professors present the image of "America the Exploiter" when they cover our foreign involvements. It does not take too much of this to create a distorted image of the United States and its culture in impressionable minds; after all, these professors are smart, aren't they? They all have Ph.Ds.

The Multicultural push in the Public School system leaves most students with no clear understanding of our national history and presents our culture as just one of many cultures and that we can learn at least as much and probably more, from other cultures. Neither the Public School system nor the colleges and universities are passing down our culture in intact form to the upcoming generations. They are presenting a distorted and an often false image that, if perpetuated, will completely phase out the Prevalent Culture and replace it with ongoing cultural conflict. After the family, the schools and the churches, the public schools colleges and universities are the primary purveyors of the culture; instead, they are destroying the culture each in their own way.

Following Is an excerpt from the Educational Resting Service's (ETS) report on American Millennials (those born after 1980) and how they measure up to their international peers.

How do the average scores of U.S. millennials compare with those in other participating countries?

In literacy, U.S. millennials scored lower than 15 of the 22 participating countries.

- In numeracy, U.S. millennials ranked last, along with Italy and Spain.

- In PS-TRE (technological subjects), U.S. millennials also ranked last, along with the Slovak Republic, Ireland, and Poland.

- The youngest segment of the U.S. millennial cohort (16- to 24-year-olds), who could be in the labor force for the next 50 years, ranked last in numeracy along with Italy and among the bottom countries in PS-TRE. In literacy, they scored higher than their peers in Italy and Spain.

How do U.S. top-performing and lower-performing millennials compare to their international peers? What is the degree of inequality in the score distribution?

- Top-scoring U.S. millennials (those at the 90th percentile) scored lower than top-scoring millennials in 15 of the 22 participating countries, and only scored higher than their peers in Spain.

- Low-scoring U.S. millennials (those at the 10th percentile) ranked last along with Italy and England/Northern Ireland and scored lower than millennials in 19 participating countries.

- The gap in scores (139 points) between U.S. millennials at the 90th and 10th percentiles was higher than the gap in 14 of the participating countries and was not significantly different than the gap in the remaining countries, signaling a high degree of inequality in the distribution of scores.

How do millennials with different levels of educational attainment perform over time and in relation to their peers internationally?

- Although a greater percentage of young adults in the U.S. are attaining higher levels of education since 2003, the numeracy scores of U.S. millennials whose highest level of education is *high school* and *above high school* have declined.

- Since 2003, the percentages of U.S. millennials scoring below level 3 in numeracy (the minimum standard) increased at all levels of educational attainment.

- U.S. millennials with a four-year bachelor's degree scored higher in numeracy than their counterparts in only two countries: Poland and Spain.

- The scores of U.S. millennials whose highest level of educational attainment was either *less than high school* or *high school* were lower than those of their counterparts in almost every other participating country.
- Our best-educated millennials—those with a master's or research degree—only scored higher than their peers in Ireland, Poland, and Spain.

What impact do demographic characteristics have on the performance of U.S. millennials?

Among all countries, there was a strong relationship between parental levels of educational attainment and skills; across all levels of parental educational attainment, there was no country where millennials scored lower than those in the United States.

- The gap in scores between U.S. millennials with the highest level of parental educational attainment and those with the lowest was among the largest of the participating countries.
- In most countries, native-born millennials scored higher than foreign-born millennials; however, native-born U.S. millennials did not perform higher than their peers in any other country.

These results should be considered against a backdrop of larger social, economic, technological, and political forces that are shaping our society. In addition, the PIAAC data suggest that simply providing more education may not hold all the answers. If, despite investments and reforms in K-12 education over the past decades, America continues to lose ground in terms of the developed skills of its adult population and workforce, then we need to better appreciate the ways in which education can perpetuate inequalities of opportunity at all educational levels, as well as help redress this problem. As a country, we need to confront not only how we can compete in a global economy, but also what kind of future we can construct when a sizable segment of our future workforce is not equipped with the skills necessary for higher-level employment and meaningful participation in our democratic institutions.

(End of ETS excerpt)

Chapter 10

The Beginnings of Cultural Self-Demolition

Three major factors come into play in a culture's pathway to self-demolition: **Mass Urbanization**.

Appeasement of the Electorate.

Excessive Population.

Democracy starts out with the best of intentions. The American experiment in Democracy was designed and implemented by some of the most brilliant minds of the late 18th and early 19th centuries -- George Washington, John Adams, Thomas Jefferson, James Madison and Benjamin Franklin, and Alexander Hamilton. They wrote a Constitution that guaranteed freedom of speech, press, religion and the right of private citizens to bear arms. Separation of Powers between the President, Congress and the Courts ensured that the country would not fall prey to dictatorship. It came with only three guarantees -- Life, Liberty and the Pursuit of happiness (opportunities for a successful life).

The United States was a predominantly agrarian society and culture when it was founded and when the Constitution was written. There were only three major cities in the entire country at that time -- Boston, New York and Philadelphia. Agrarian societies are small and rural making them more conducive and receptive to traditional American values -- self-reliance, limited government and a Free Market economy. On the farm and in rural small businesses, everyone is expected to carry their share of the load. Rural communities take care of themselves and resent outside (government) interference. In agrarian communities everyone earns their living by the fruits of their labor. Nothing is free.

Once you move to the city you learn dependency. You depend on the municipal government to provide electricity, running water and sewers. In the country people were able to survive without those amenities to a large extent. In the urban structure they are essential necessities. In the urban environment you rely on a wide variety of public services; in addition to electricity, water and sewers you are dependent on police and fire departments, public transportation, public education, and public maintenance to keep the infrastructure in good repair. You are also dependent on an employer for a job. In the country and small towns you made your own living working for yourself or your family or a reliable employer in town who you could trust to be there. In the city you were subject to economic cycles and employers who really did not care about you like good old Mr. Whipple back at the Rock Creek General Store.

Family support was often missing for those who moved away from rural Americana into the cities to take advantage of the Industrial Revolution, a major driver of American urbanization. So, it was no coincidence or surprise that Social Security, Unemployment Insurance and AFDC were well received by the urban population but considered "charity" in the rural areas that looked down on "free money" as contributing to laziness and indolence.

Today, urban areas are overwhelmingly Secular Progressive. They are centers of support for the Secular Progressive agenda -- abortion, same sex marriage; physician assisted suicide and legalized drugs. There is little support for traditional American values in urban America today. There is still support for them in those parts of the country that have a more rural and agrarian population. The population of the country is increasingly urban, especially on the two coasts. These areas overwhelmingly vote Secular Progressive (Democrat). The primary molders of opinion -- the universities, the major media outlets and the entertainment industry are all located in heavily urbanized regions. The major urban areas support Big Government, massive Entitlement programs, open borders and the Secular progressive social agenda that are out of synch with traditional values. Church attendance is lower in urban than in rural and agrarian America.

Urban residents, as a group, are willing to allow more government control and intervention in their lives as long as government delivers the Entitlements. Urban areas have large concentrations of Protected Groups who favor more government control in return for meeting their needs and catering to their agendas. Regional voting trends bear this out. Agrarian areas have migrant workers but they are often transients; however, agrarian regions with permanent resident populations of Hispanics (or other minorities) will become more progressive.

+++

As Democracy evolves it becomes increasingly hostage to the often uninformed demands and desires of the electorate-- the people who put the politicians in office. The government is more willing to sacrifice its long term interests, including national security interests, in favor of the short term demands of the electorate. We saw this in the 1930s when governments in the United States and Europe ignored the rise of Nazi Germany and Imperial Japan because their populations were war weary from World War I. Those international problems that could have been resolved quickly with decisive action during the mid-1930s exploded into World War II in the 1940s.

Today the world is making the same mistake with Radical Islam. World leaders know that this problem will only increase and worsen but could be stopped with quick and decisive military action now but the people, *the electorate*, does not want war so once again we will wait until it is almost too late; and with nuclear weapons now in the equation, it may already be too late when World War III breaks out. Social Democratic Europe is afraid of its Muslim population and works hard to appease it so taking any kind of decisive action is not an option for Europe.

An agrarian based society is more apt to accept and support a need for military action since the war could be sold to them based on their value system. Historically, it has always been easier to recruit soldiers from agrarian regions than urban centers. Urban residents are accustomed to an easier way of life and don't want to deal with the hardships of war. During the Civil War, resistance to the military draft was centered in urban areas, particularly New York City. The farm boys were more willing to serve.

A monarchy or a dictatorship would not hesitate to take all means necessary for national defense and survival. That's why the ancient empires lasted as long as they did and when they did fall they were conquered by a stronger military power; they did not collapse from placating a population that was unwilling to make the sacrifices necessary for survival. Rome was an exception to this rule since, although it was a monarchy, the rulers were afraid of upsetting a massive population that could have rebelled. The Roman population, toward the end of the Empire, was unwilling to exert itself and the emperors were willing to appease them with "bread and circuses" and to outsource their military to the barbarians from the fringes of the Empire who would eventually bring it down.

In the present day, a monarchy or dictatorship with full power would declare war on Radical Islam and deport the Muslims within its boundaries. Such action is nearly impossible in a modern democracy because of the social and moral image this would generate as well as the complexities of Due Process in the Democratic system.

Democracy eventually leads to a paralysis of will as governments become fearful of taking any kind of action that would anger the electorate and result in a loss on Election Day. This is happening now in both Europe and the United States.

The theorem of this chapter is that mass urbanization is the beginning of the end for democracy. The next step is appeasement through disregard of national security interests combined with massive increases in Entitlement spending that will eventually lead to national bankruptcy. Money is a finite resource that will eventually run out or become so devalued that it will be worthless. This happened in Germany during the 1920s.

+++

Genuine democracy can survive only in small entities. This raises the question: Is the United States too big to function effectively as a culture and a society? We hit the 200 million mark in 1968, around the time the country started the long, slow, agonizing process of unravelling. Today we are over 300 million. It is impossible to get an accurate count due to the large number of people who are here illegally with no way to track them. Large national populations create problems similar to large urban areas -- feelings of anomie and isolation, a bigger demand for public services, and diverse constituencies with different needs, demands and agendas. Government begins exerting more control and interference under the guise of protecting, defending and supporting the population. The greater the population, the greater number of groups politicians pander to and appease. Large populations become polarized based on their ethnicities, interests and agendas. You have to look no further than India, the world's largest democracy, to see what an exercise in chaos that country has become with Sikhs, Hindus, Muslims, Christians and others -- all with conflicting interests, agendas -- and languages. When you have large diverse populations you invariably have different languages. Lack of an official language further Balkanizes and fragments a country.

Smaller entities are always easier to manage whether they are a family, a company, a corporation, or a nation. Dictatorships can control large countries and empires with diverse populations longer since they use brute force but even they collapse eventually. Two examples are ancient Rome and the Soviet Union in our own time. The best managed countries have been small and homogeneous in population; Sweden with 9. 6 million, Norway with 5.6 million, Denmark with 5.6 million, and Finland with 5.5 million. A homogenous culture and one language were unifying factors but in recent years the large influx of Muslim immigrants has been causing social upheaval and disruption in these countries diluting their cultural and linguistic unity.

Chapter 11

Why Some Cultures Never Expand

Four areas that come to mind are sub-Saharan Africa, the North American Indians, the Australian Aborigines, and Middle Eastern Bedouins. Sub-Saharan Africa was colonized by England, France, Belgium, and the White Afrikaners in South Africa. The result was that the indigenous peoples were, to a large extent, "Europeanized" by the colonial powers. The North American Indians were similarly absorbed into the North American culture as were the Aborigines by the Australians. These groups retained many aspects of their native cultures but, for all intents and purposes, became Europeanized, Americanized, and Australianized in their cultural pillars. Bedouins were an Islamic culture but moved freely around the Middle East owing no national allegiance (unless they settled permanently in one area) and living according to their own customs.

These cultures all share a common characteristic; they are tribal. Tribal cultures are historically primitive with their main occupation being survival. Their political system was limited to tribal leadership. Tribal economics was the barter system since they did not develop their own currency or coinage. Tribes had no organized military. Every able bodied male was a warrior. Most of these tribes had no written alphabet and handed down their traditions and culture though storytellers who orally transmitted their traditions and stories. Religion was animistic and pagan (except for the Bedouins). Each tribe may have had their own god or family of gods or may have shared gods with neighboring tribes. The American Indians had a concept of a "Great Spirit" as well as other animistic sub-deities. There was no organized doctrine or theology. Their language may have been local or shared with other nearby tribes. Middle Eastern Bedouins share a common language (Arabic) and religion (Islam).

Tribes never were able to build the six cultural pillars and develop the institutions needed for cultural growth, development and expansion. These tribes developed some excellent traditions that placed emphasis on honor, hospitality, and friendship but they lived in harsh geographic and climatic environments and were distrustful of and often hostile toward other tribes and outsiders.

This was the case in Saudi Arabia until King Abdulaziz united the region by marrying women from all the tribes on the peninsula thus creating a royal family that included all of the previously warring tribes. He made a nation out of of warring Bedouin tribes and he did it with British and American assistance which helped create modern Saudi Arabia's political, military and economic pillars.

An interesting question: how did the Aztecs, Mayans, and Incas develop such a high level of civilization? They probably had contact with civilizations like the Egyptians and Chinese. How else did Mesoamerican Indians conceive of the idea of pyramids? Mummified remains in Egypt contain traces of drugs indigenous to Central and South America. If the invading Spaniards had not destroyed so much information from those cultures we may have a record of transoceanic contacts. The Central and South American Indian tribes benefited from contact with advanced cultures thereby advancing their own. There is no other explanation for their higher levels of civilization as opposed to the North American tribes' mostly primitive tribal cultures.

Chapter 12

A House Divided

Matthew 12:25

"And Jesus knowing their thoughts, said to them: Every kingdom divided against itself shall be made desolate: and every city or house *divided against itself* shall not stand."

Mark 3:24

"And if a kingdom be *divided against itself*, that kingdom cannot stand."

The United States has been a severely polarized nation since the mid-1960s and the degree of polarization is getting worse. We are divided along five major fault lines any one of which could fracture the country into Balkanized fragments:

Struggle between Traditional Americans and Secular Progressives.

Hyper-partisanship between the two political parties.

Race Relations

Language

Generational Gaps

If one thing is clear from reading this book, it is the divide between Traditional Americans who are trying to maintain traditional American values and Secular Progressives who view those values as "survival of the fittest" devices the White (male) majority uses to keep minorities and women "in their place." Secular Progressives want to dump self-reliance, limited government and Free Market economics in favor of European Social Democracy.

+++

The two political parties have taken sides resulting in government gridlock making it almost impossible to pass legislation. The two parties cannot seem to work together or agree on anything. That hyper partisanship was emphasized when Former Senate Majority leader, Harry Reid, chuckled in an interview with CNN about lying when he alleged that 2012 Republican presidential candidate, Mitt Romney, had not paid any federal income taxes in years. When the reporter asked him how he felt about that, Reid smiled and said: "He didn't win, did he?"

++

Race relations between Blacks and Whites are deteriorating. Race relations had been getting better since the 1970s. In those days we had television shows such as *All in the Family, The Jeffersons, Good Times,* and *Sanford and Son* where we could laugh and kid about racial differences. You would think that electing a Black president would have helped improve race relations even more but it has had just the opposite effect; any criticism of President Obama's policies are labeled racist. Blacks keep calling for a national discussion about race relations but if Whites bring up topics like the disintegration of the Black family they are immediately labeled as racists and not only by Blacks but by White Secular Progressives in the media. Any time a White expresses a difference of opinion with a Black, he is labeled a racist thereby effectively ending the discussion. Race relations between Blacks and Whites are at an impasse in this country today. There are many exceptions to this at the individual level but at the collective level it is not good.

Blacks and Whites have become two separate cultures co-existing in one country. We have separate music and entertainment cultures, a different linguistic culture and many in the younger generation of Blacks have names that are a blend of African and American cultures. There is, for want of a better term, a form of *voluntary* segregation. Black and White adults don't socialize much together beyond the work place or school. They usually get along well in those venues but go their separate ways at closing time. There are no more segregated neighborhoods but you still do not see many Black families in predominantly White neighborhoods.

We seemed to be coming together as a nation in the years immediately following the Civil Rights Movement but we have grown further apart. There seems to be two causes for this: **(1)** The development of a distinctly Black American culture -- language, music, entertainment, and worldview; **(2)** A "leadership" that keeps telling Blacks that their problems aren't their fault but the fault of the White majority who keep the Black community down through denial of opportunities for economic advancement making it difficult, if not impossible, for them to succeed in America.

((AUTHOR'S NOTE: We have cited examples in this book where Whites have been destroyed due to racial remarks while Blacks can make some of the most vicious statements imaginable about Whites with no public outrage from Whites or Blacks. Black reaction to White remarks is usually way out of proportion to what was actually said and is selective: No Black outrage over the caricature of Condoleeza Rice with big lips and buck teeth or when Rutgers made it clear they did not want her as a Commencement speaker, no outrage when NPR fired Juan Williams for an honest comment about being apprehensive over obvious Muslims on airplanes. Williams was referred to as FOX NEWS' "Happy Negro" by another Black, Syracuse University professor Boyce Watkins , and no outrage over frequent attacks on Supreme Court Justice Clarence Thomas by White Liberals.

Some Blacks seem to be looking for reasons to take offense at Whites; either that or they have been convinced by influential members of their community that Whites still hate them and are out to get them.   This issue needs to be the topic of an open national discussion. The alternative could be increasing violence such as the tragedy at the Black Church in Charleston, South Carolina where a White Supremacist killed nine people at a prayer meeting. As of now no one wants to acknowledge the existence of this smoldering cultural volcano. We have come to a cultural crossroads in race relations and it needs to be addressed and discussed in the public forum since it is fueling cultural decline in this country for all of us. There are too many fine people in both communities to allow this to continue.)

The racial divide is currently in the spotlight with the *Black Lives Matter* movement. This group came together in the wake of recent police shootings of Blacks during confrontations. They have vowed to disrupt the Republican National Convention next year. They told a White reporter that he wasn't welcome to cover them since their meeting was for Blacks only. When Martin O'Malley, former Governor of Maryland, who is running for the Democratic presidential nomination, addressed them, he said "ALL Lives matter." This angered the audience and O'Malley apologized. (See Author's Note below.) This organization seems think that only

Black lives matter and only when they are killed by a White person; in other words, the fact that most young Blacks who die violently are killed by other young Blacks does not seem to matter; nor does it seem to bother this crowd when a nine month old baby is killed by a stray bullet in Detroit while sleeping on a couch, or a little girl is killed while riding her tricycle in south Chicago, or a nine year old girl in Ferguson, Missouri is killed by another stray bullet sitting on her mother's bed doing her schoolwork. This crowd is only focused on Whites, particularly the police who are risking their lives every day to keep what is left of the threadbare social fabric of the inner cities from completely unraveling into anarchy. But they have no problem taking "White" money from George Soros who is helping to bankroll this outfit.

Movements like Black Lives Matter only exacerbate racial tensions in this country. Fortunately, most Blacks reject that kind of extremism but it reflects on the Black community as a whole just as the Charleston murders reflected on the White Community as a whole. This has got to stop and we have to come together since we are all in this together as a culture and a people.

(AUTHOR'S NOTE: Apologizing to "offended" lunatics is a form of Political Correctness that needs to go away; and, like Political Correctness, which also needs to go away, it has become too deeply embedded in the cultural psyche.)

+++

We have already discussed the consequences of multiple languages in a culture. We need an Official Language. We used to (and still do) have neighborhoods where you would rarely hear a word of English. There is nothing wrong with that but when residents of these neighborhoods are looking for jobs, utilizing public services and attending school they need to be proficient in English. Nothing will break up a culture faster than multiple "official" languages. The Tower of Babel (Genesis: 11: 1-9) is a cautionary tale about this. The Scriptures say that *they were one people because they spoke one language*.("And the Lord said: Truly they are one people and they all speak the same language." Genesis 11:6) When they started speaking multiple languages they were scattered all over the earth. ("…the Lord confused their speech…and scattered them all over the earth." Genesis 11: 8) Multiple languages have that effect on a culture.

++

We first heard the term "Generation Gap" during the Hippie movement in the 1960s. This term was coined to describe the gulf in values between the Baby Boomers, those born during the immediate post-World War II years, and their parents' generation. The Baby Boomers had it much easier growing up than their parents and grandparents due to the unparalleled economic prosperity and technological development the country enjoyed during the post-war era. More Boomers went to college than any previous generation and this included many more females.

As we discussed in chapter 5, the 1950s developed no moral capital of its own; instead, it survived on the moral capital of the pre-war culture. That fact coupled with having life handed to them on a silver platter was not a character building combination. Parents who came up experiencing the hardships of the Great Depression and World War II wanted to give their children all the things they never had. This gave the Boomers a feeling of "entitlement" while the political and social upheavals of the 1960s (race riots, anti- Vietnam War demonstrations and avant-garde attitudes about sex and drugs) made them feel superior to the "outdated" moral codes of their parents. The parents of the Boomer generation were as much to blame as the kids themselves. They still held to traditional values but did a poor job of passing them on to their children. Mom and Dad were too busy acquiring material goodies and "keeping up with the Joneses" and this rubbed off on their children. Instead of passing on traditional values as parents had done in the past, the Boomer parents passed on a love of materialism and an easy lifestyle; to many of these Boomers, that meant "me first."

This had a domino effect. If marriage wasn't like what they had seen in 1950s television programs or the love stories crooned by Do-Op troubadours, they would just get a divorce. Boomer women wanted "to have it all" -- a family and a career -- and their children would be raised by daycare nannies with parents having less time due to the demands of the job and their busy lifestyles to pay attention to their children.

The 1970s and beyond witnessed the rise of the single-parent family since it was now acceptable, thanks to the sexual mores first practiced by the Boomers in the 1960s, to have children out of wedlock. There was no stigma attached to that anymore; in fact, the single mom was a heroine. By the late 1980s half of America's children were either living in single parent homes or with one biological parent and one step-parent or a biological mother hosting a series of temporary boyfriends.

The Millennial generation (those born after 1980) is the first generation to come of age with almost no connection to traditional American culture. They live in an artificial world of Facebook, Twitter, Instachat, Snapchat, texting, cell phones and other kinds of gadgetry Luddites like myself are not familiar with (and don't want to be familiar with). They have no interest in what came before them in the culture; part of that is due to the terrible job the public schools have done in teaching History and Civics. They are totally immersed in their gadgets and technology -- it's all about living in the moment. They have no grasp of the past. A young lady who was on my caseload when I worked for Washington State told me that her father "was in the war." When n asked her which war she had no idea. "I don't know," she replied. "He was just in the war."

Support for Traditional values has been slipping since the Boomers came of age in the 1960s. The Millennial generation is socially libertarian, totally accepting of same sex marriage, out-of-wedlock births, unmarried couples living together and having children together, physician assisted suicide and legalized drugs. Most Millennials I encounter have out-of-wedlock children or are living with someone who has them. Case in point: Three Millennials, all males, who work at a cafe I frequent, are all living with their girlfriends aka fiancées. Two have children with these girls and one is expecting a baby. The latter's gal pal has another child from a previous relationship. This is the new normal. One more generation of this and marriage will be a novelty, an exception or at best, an afterthought.

Millennials smoke marijuana like previous generations smoked cigarettes. There is growing support for a social democratic style of government among Millennials that will take care of everything womb to tomb. This demographic votes overwhelmingly Democratic-- no surprise there.

162

Traditional American values have been on the wane since the Baby Boomer generation and each subsequent generation has drifted further and further away from those values. This was underscored in a 2011 Pew Research poll -- just 32 percent of Millennials believe the U.S. is the greatest country in the world. That number progressively increases among the Gen X (48%), Boomer (50%) and Silent generations (64%). The Millennial generation is pivotal in that they have not consciously or deliberately rejected traditional values, but that they never had those values conveyed to them by parents, schools and churches. The Millennials, as a group, are aware of them only as abstract concepts, not something they grew up hearing about every day or seeing portrayed in movies and on television. These media stopped promoting traditional American values decades ago.

The most disturbing element in this generational equation is that those on the extreme ends of the generational spectrum -- what's left of "The Greatest Generation" and the Silent Generation (those who came of age during the Great Depression and World War II) and the oldest Baby Boomers on one end, and Millennials on the other -- have nothing in common. Older people may know how to use a computer, surf the internet, do e-mail and use a Smart Phone but many of us cannot relate to Facebook, Twitter, Instagram and all the different "apps" available for download. Fifty years ago, the generations shared a common culture. All age groups were familiar with the famous movie and entertainment celebrities. I can remember talking and interacting freely with adults when I was in grade school. We were on the same page in technology -- we all could dial a telephone and knew which knobs did what on the black and white television. We all knew how to work a reel-to-reel tape recorder and we could talk about current events since I and most of my friends read newspapers and had current events classes in grade school as early as second grade. Every week beginning in second grade we had to present reports out of newspapers. Millennials are low information. This has had a negative impact on critical thinking skills which you really don't need if all you're doing is pushing buttons on some kind of machine or device.

A sadder manifestation of the growing generational gap is the diminished relationship between grandparents and grandchildren. This is because grandparents and grandchildren operate out of different cultural paradigms so there is less to talk about between generations than there was a few decades ago. Baby Boomers were the last generation who collectively revered, enjoyed and appreciated grandparents because the generational experiences were more similar and were more easily transmitted, shared and enjoyed.

The Millennials represent the fulfillment of a cultural transformation that began in the 1960s. This new culture is based on technology and moral relativism. This is the culture that will be carried forward by the Millennials and their children.

The Millennials are a totally different version of American culture than previous generations; unless there is a cultural sea change of some kind, the Millennials represent the New America.

One final observation on the Millennial generation-- and this could apply to all post Baby Boomers to a certain extent as well since this trend had its beginnings with them: softness in the males and harshness in the females.. I admit that this is a *completely anecdotal* observation but I find agreement in this assessment with most people in my generation when I bring up the topic. Young twentysomething men and women are somehow different than we were when my generation was in that age group. Millennial males are the products of a culture that sent out a lot of subliminal messages, and some not so subliminal, that male characteristics were violent, abusive and patriarchal. They have been conditioned by society to be quieter and meeker. This is, I admit, a highly generalized statement, but think about it as you observe young males in today's society-- while not being feminized per se, they have become less masculine in the traditional sense f the word. Their upbringing was softer. The schools could not yell at them, berate them or use corporal punishment. Military basic training was modified somewhat to be less harsh and abrasive. For a while, some branches of the military issued "stress cards" that a basic trainee could pull out if the drill sergeant was coming on too strong. As a result of this kinder, gentler society, so many young soldiers are suffering from PTSD and have a higher suicide rate than veterans of previous generations. The World War II and Korean War veterans witnessed a lot of horror and internalized it but their disciplined and structured upbringing by no nonsense parents and schools -- and seriously no nonsense military training -- combined with the hardships of the Great Depression, instilled an intestinal fortitude that is missing today. We cannot cite definitive studies on this phenomenon since it is still in the process of unfolding, but deep within ourselves we know that the Millennial male generation is not the John Wayne generation. Vietnam veterans returned with a host of problems resulting from their wartime experience with much of that brought on by drugs that were plentiful in Vietnam thanks to the North Vietnamese; however, part of it was linked to the soft childhood of the 1950s and the narcissism of the 1960s.

Another factor is the blurred roles of the genders over the past few decades both at home and in the workplace. Where men and women previously had clearly defined roles, that is no longer the case and this has led to gender role confusion. As we have already seen, this has strengthened the female image (not always in the best ways) and weakened the male.

(AUTHOR'S NOTE: I looked for some empirical studies to back up my theory on the feminization of men and, like my own, there is anecdotal material out there. I have already referenced the best two scholarly studies in this area, *The War on Boys* by Christina Hoff Sommers and *Men on Strike* by Helen Smith, Ph.D. We can expect more solid research on this topic as time goes on.)

None of this means that the Millennial generation or the Baby Boomers are inherently weak. They are the products of their culture and their upbringing. The Millennials have not been trained in self-sufficiency which is evidenced by the large numbers (one-third according to some studies) who live at home well into their 20s and sometimes beyond. When my father was laid off at Goodyear Tire & Rubber in Akron in 1938, my grandparents staked him to a train ticket out to Seattle (an opportunity) since the economy was better there. My grandfather told him that they were not going to support an able bodied man with no family. Then Dad got the "if you can pick up a broom you can eat" lecture. He was told to "write when you get work" as in "we're not sending you any money so don't send us any begging letters." When Dad arrived in Seattle he got a job as a soda jerk at the Twin Teepees restaurant across from Green Lake (where he met my mom who was working as a waitress there). Today's Millennials need that kind of life experience.

Millennial women on the other hand appear more aggressive and abrasive -- more willing to get "in your face." They too have been conditioned by a culture that believes women were treated like second class citizens and expected to be submissive, so they were encouraged to exhibit more masculine characteristics. What happened is that they are displaying the worst of male characteristics, that of the jerk. Women today can be brutally competitive in the work place. Most of my female co-workers said they preferred to have a male supervisor since men were not as competitive and back stabbing. (In other words, were male supervisors become more feminized while the female bosses were becoming more masculine?) Like my observations concerning Millennial males, my thoughts on Millennial females are anecdotal rather than empirical facts.

Here's the closest I can come to empirical evidence for this theorem: Ever see two men fight; ever see two women fight? I rest my case.

I don't mean to be hard on Millennials. I've liked most of the Millennials I've interacted with. They are a product of their culture, a culture that evolved, like all cultures evolve-- through a set of historical circumstances. If you took a Millennial living at home staring at his hand held device playing video games and transplanted him back into a pre-World War II home environment, he would have been an exemplary representative of the Greatest Generation. If my Dad were 22 today and got laid off he'd be living at home indefinitely on his dad's dime and his dad's health insurance; same two people, same two cultures. Had my dad or our hypothetical Millennial grown up in Nazi Germany and been saturated with that culture, they may have ended up as concentration camp guards at Auschwitz. We are all formed and influenced by our culture and that includes our individual personalities. It is the culture that drives these changes within us much more than individual choice. It could be called "cultural pressure" which is a form of peer pressure but more subtle and opaque-- and all encompassing.

Chapter 13

A Culture is Driven by Its Own Unique Philosophy

All cultures are defined by their cultural philosophy. It may be something as basic as conquest and expansion. These defined the ancient Middle Eastern empires (Egypt, Assyria, Babylon, and Persia). It may be some crazy belief in the superiority of one society over another (Nazi Germany and its Master Race doctrine) or it may also be some vague concept like Soviet Russia's "Dictatorship of the Proletariat" which was nothing more than an enigmatic obfuscation for conquest and expansion hidden behind a perverted social justice fig leaf. Ancient Greece had a number of cultural philosophies depending upon which city state you lived in. Sparta was pure militarism. Athens was the *Polis* -- a democracy governed by philosophers and intellectuals. Much of our western political and intellectual structure derived from the Athenian philosophers -- Socrates, Aristotle and Plato.

There have been four major cultural philosophies in the West besides the Athenian polis.

1. Ancient Rome, when it was a Republic, operated under the philosophy of *Pietas*. This was the guiding philosophy of the Roman Republic from its origin in 509 B.C. until the time of the Caesars. It was not *piety* as the Latin would imply, but rather a sense of honor best described by a phrase that once defined America: "My word is my bond." In times of national emergency the Roman Senate, the governing body of the Roman Republic, would turn full power over to a citizen recognized for his wisdom, virtue, and Pietas for a period of six months. At the end of the six months the Dictator, as he was called, was expected to relinquish all power back to the Senate. Some dictators relinquished power earlier -- as soon as the crisis had passed. *Dictator* meant *ruler*, not tyrant, as it does today.

The greatest exemplar of Pietas was Marcus Atilius Regulus, a Roman General in the First Punic War (c. 250 B.C.) who was captured by the Carthaginians. The Carthaginians sent him back to Rome to negotiate a peace treaty on the grounds that he would return to Carthage. Regulus returned to Rome but persuaded the Roman Senate NOT to negotiate peace. Then, true to his word, he returned to Carthage where he was tortured to death. He was safe in Rome and did not have to go back to Carthage. But, due to the virtue and philosophy of Pietas, he did knowing full well that he would be killed and not painlessly either.

Pietas disappeared with the Caesars but Rome survived on the accumulated capital of Pietas until 180 A.D., the year the Roman Emperor Marcus Aurelius died. Marcus Aurelius was, arguably, the last Roman Emperor who practiced the ancient virtues. They had already disappeared among the Roman people. Today, the moral capital of the past is consumed at a much faster rate in direct proportion to material and technical progress. Material progress was much slower in ancient times. The Roman soldiers wore basically the same armor and equipment in 400 A.D. that they had worn in 400 B.C. But when the accumulated capital of Pietas finally expired, Rome went into decline because its defining philosophy was no longer there to sustain and support it. Pietas was replaced by "Bread and Circuses."

2.   The successor of the ancient Roman Empire was the Holy Roman Empire which lasted through various metamorphoses until 1918 when its final incarnation, the Austro-Hungarian Empire was defeated in World War I. The defining philosophy of the Holy Roman Empire was *Christendom* which meant the Catholic Faith. All of the institutions of the Holy Roman Empire -- the secular administration, the Papacy, the universities, and the military -- were dedicated to preserving the Catholic Religion.

The Holy Roman Empire went into decline at the beginning of the Protestant Reformation. Its influence continually shrank and it is questionable when the Holy Roman Empire officially disappeared but the Austro-Hungarian Empire was the last confessional state in Europe that held to Christendom. The Catholic Church was more than a State Church (e.g., the Church of England), it was the defining philosophy of the Empire. The Austro-Hungarian Emperor had veto power over Papal elections and he did veto the original outcome of the 1903 Papal election that would have made Cardinal Mariano Rampolla Pope. Rampolla was believed to be a Freemason or at last to have a close association with the Order (there were other political issues as well) so the Emperor, Franz Joseph, vetoed Rampolla clearing the way for (Giuseppe Sarto) Pope St. Pius X.

3.   The defining Philosophy of the United States was *limited government and self-reliance enshrined in the Free Market system.* Since big government destroys self-reliance, the Founders opted for limited government. The idea was to provide opportunity for economic success and prosperity-- not a guarantee. This is why so many Europeans came to America up though the early 20th century -- opportunities that were not available in Europe.

The decline of America began in the late 1960s when the government started following the same path as Western Europe. (See below.) With the speed of material progress and technology, we have all but exhausted the accumulated cultural capital of self-reliance and limited government.

4.   Western Europe decided to counteract that lack of opportunity with guaranteed security through Social Democracy. This system guarantees economic security through generous welfare and unemployment entitlements, free medical care, free education, and generous pensions. Europe has been a sucker for this kind of system in some form or other since the mid-19th century (Fabian Socialism, the thinking of Karl Marx) and it manifested itself in the extreme though Soviet Communism and German National Socialism (Nazism).

Social Democracy has never built any residual capital because it requires nothing from the individual. It meets all needs by handing out benefits enabling total dependency on the government. This system will enable poverty since it is fully dependent on a viable tax base, a tax base that is disappearing through a declining birth rate and an increasing geriatric population that will siphon more and more money out of the system. Social Democracy is crumbling under its own weight in southern Europe. Greece is financially dependent on the European Union refusing to cut back on generous pension benefits and other Entitlements that it cannot afford but cannot do away with because the Greek people have become addicted to them. (As of this writing, Greece is receiving its third bailout and has agreed to raise taxes and cut benefits. We'll see.) It is only a matter of time before the erosion spreads up north. Social Democracy has already done major economic damage to Italy, Spain and Portugal with high rates of unemployment and unmanageable and unsustainable debt.

A few years ago I was talking to a man at the airport who was on his way to Denmark to take a teaching position in a college in Copenhagen. He wanted to get in on some of that Social Democracy. He admitted that the cost of living was high but he didn't care because "the government takes care of everything so there is no incentive to save." One slight problem with that rationale: What happens when the government has to start cutting back on the Entitlements or goes bankrupt?

Social Democracy does not sustain a viable culture and inspires no virtue because it's always "me first." Virtue is a product of personal responsibility while Social Democracy gives everything freely and requires no responsibility for obtaining these benefits. The only sense of sacrifice may be in the taxation but if that becomes too much of a burden just go on the dole. It has all but destroyed religious faith since there is no perceived need for faith in God anymore. "We've got the government so who needs God?" (There is more to it than that but the false guarantees of Social Democracy contribute to religious decline by promoting a false sense of security.)

The United States Government is in the process of replacing self-reliance and limited government with a European model that expects nothing except tax money from its citizens. In the United States half of the population pays no taxes anyway so taxation is only required from higher income earners.

When parents give their children everything and expect nothing in return they create irresponsible children with a feeling of entitlement who are unwilling to contribute anything to the family and it is the same with free government benefits. When the government does that, the culture dies.

The present crisis of cultural decline can be summed up in the following quote attributed to Alexander Tyler, a professor of History at the University of Edinburgh during the late 18th century. He had this to say about democracy: "A democracy is always temporary in nature; it simply cannot exist as a permanent form of government. A democracy will continue to exist until the time that voters discover that they can vote themselves generous benefits from the public treasury. From that moment on, the majority always votes for the candidates who promise the most benefits from the public treasury, with the result that every democracy will finally collapse over loose fiscal policy, (which is) always followed by a dictatorship."

That is similar to what Ayn Rand said in the 1950s: "The only difference between the Welfare state and a totalitarian dictatorship is a matter of time."

Chapter 14

Historical Epochs

America's cultural decline is part of a larger worldwide crumbling. A similar unravelling is taking place in Europe. The Islamic State of Iraq and Syria is in competition with Iran as to who will be the dominant power in the Middle East. Whichever of those two powers wins will eventually rule the Middle East. Russia is trying to take over The Ukraine with the ultimate goal of restoring the former Soviet Union. China is becoming the major military power in the Far East threatening regional stability. China is constructing islands on coral reefs in the South China Sea with obvious military purposes. Iran is working on developing a nuclear bomb with the clearly stated intention of destroying Israel. The United States, Canada, Europe, Australia, Asia and Africa are under constant threat of terrorist attacks.

There is no leadership in North America or Europe that is effectively standing up to Islamic Radicalism and Russian and Chinese expansionism. The United States government refuses to use the term *Islamic Jihad* or *radical Islam* or any other term that effectively defines the threat; as we have already seen, the government prefer terms like "workplace violence."

As you look around the world the benevolent -- or at least once benevolent powers -- are all in decline while the malevolent powers are on the rise.

All of the problems the world is experiencing now are signs of epochal collapse. By *epochal* we mean a historical period -- a historical epoch.

The current epoch can mark the beginning of its collapse with the outbreak of World War II. This led to the end of the European colonial period since the European colonial powers were so weakened by two world wars that they no longer had the resources and manpower to maintain their colonies in Africa, Asia and the Middle East. This left a power vacuum in those regions that would be filled by unstable regimes. The one power in the world with the ability to maintain order was the United States but it came under the increasing control of Secular Progressives who wanted no part of foreign intervention and were determined to transform the country into a European Social Democracy focused on entitlement, not military spending.

When we did fight foreign wars -- Korea, Vietnam, Iraq and Afghanistan -- we fought them with the emphasis on politics and not military victory. Since World War II we have fought major conflicts in Korea, Vietnam, Kuwait, Afghanistan and Iraq. We broke even in Korea nd Kuwait. We saved South Korea and Kuwait from their invaders but left the invading powers intact in their own countries (North Korea and Iraq). We lost in Vietnam and Iraq by pulling out and leaving those countries without any military support -- a residual force of American ground troops. Iran now controls four Arab capitals -- Baghdad, Damascus, Sana'a and Beirut. ISIS controls half of Syria and one third of Iraq. Libya has had no functioning government since we helped overthrow Muammar Gaddafi and then walked away from the mess that we helped create. ISIS is filling in that power vacuum in Libya. Russia poses a threat to the Baltic States, Moldavia and what is left of the Ukraine. Cultural divisions plague Europe and North America (See chapter 7). There is no part of the world today that is free from threat of attack from hostile forces.

We are now in the Fifth Epoch of recorded history. The First Epoch lasted from 3000 B.C. to 330 B.C. when Alexander the Great conquered Persia. For the previous 2700 years the balance of power was held by the great Middle Eastern empires -- Egypt, Assyria, Babylon and Persia. India and China dominated the Far East. The Second Epoch was the Greco-Roman period which lasted from 330 B.C. to 410 A,D., the fall of the Roman Empire in the West. The Third Epoch was the early Middle Ages (5th century A.D. to the 12th century A.D.) controlled by the Holy Roman Empire in the West and Constantinople in the East. The Fourth Epoch was the High Middle Ages (13th to 15th centuries) which saw the rise of England, France and the Italian city states. This was the era of the Renaissance. It ended in the later part of the 15th century with the fall of Constantinople to the Muslim Turks in 1453 A.D. and the further rise of England and France. Spain threw off Moorish domination in 1492 A.D. with the fall of the last Muslim stronghold at Granada.

The Fifth Epoch began around 1500 with the expansion of England, France and Spain. All would become colonial powers over the next few centuries dominating North and South America, Africa and Asia including India. Belgium and Portugal would become lesser colonial powers but powers nonetheless. Turkey rose to dominance in the Middle East during this epoch; after World War I, Britain and France took over the Turkish colonies in the Middle East. The greatest event of the Fifth Epoch was the founding and rise of the United States which would be instrumental in destroying Nazism and bringing down Soviet Communism ending them as international threats. The Fifth Epoch witnessed the end of absolute monarchy in the West and the rise of the Democratic system of government. The Fifth Epoch has lasted a little over 500 years and we do not know how much longer it can hold on but it is clear that the world is bracing for another epochal change.

The First and Second Epochs came to violent and abrupt ends. The transition between the Third, Fourth and Fifth Epochs was smoother in that there was no massive disruption and upheaval except for the fall of Constantinople which gave rise to Turkey as a world power that would threaten Europe. Two of those threats would be imminent and narrowly averted; 1572 with the defeat of the Turkish Navy at the Battle of Lepanto and 1683 when King John Sobieski of Poland broke the Turkish siege of Vienna. Turkey sided with Germany and Austria-Hungary against the United States, England, France and Russia in World War I. Being on the losing side of that conflict ended their empire. At the height of its power, Turkey controlled portions of southeastern Europe along with most of the Middle East.

The current historical Epoch, the Fifth Epoch, will probably end in a global conflict between Islam and the West with China siding with Islam and Russia most likely siding with the West since they already have problems with radical Mjuslims in their own territory. Whoever wins that global conflict will determine the course of the Sixth Epoch. Assuming the West will win, we can predict that the balance of power will shift back toward Europe and the form of government will be monarchy or dictatorship since, if the West does win, it will take strong central leadership to ensure victory and that will most likely carry over after the conflict is ended. Democracy will be seen as a failure since democracy and its inherent weaknesses (Entitlement programs that lead to bankruptcy and social agendas that cause moral decline)

174

contributed to the worldwide conflagration that collapsed the Fifth Epoch. There will be enormous loss of life in this worldwide war and the Sixth Epoch will see a religious renaissance accompanied by more respect for authority since authority was a key factor in victory -- not the Political Correctness and appeasement that had come to characterize and define democracy. During times of great upheaval and chaos, people return to their religious roots.

It is difficult to forecast the role of the United States in the Sixth Epoch. The United States no longer exercises and provides leadership and if the leadership emerges out of Europe during the global war, then Europe will be the leading power during the Sixth Epoch.

The Islamic world is currently in a state of turmoil but it is consolidating its power in the Middle East. The only factor that is preventing it from launching all-out war against the West NOW is the division between Sunni and Shia Muslims. ISIS is radical Sunni and Iran is radical Shia. The wealthy Gulf oil states are Sunni but fear the radicalism of ISIS. ISIS has a clearly stated goal of invading Europe and "conquering Rome." Both ISIS and Iran want to wipe Israel off the map and eventually destroy the United States. It is only a matter of time before these quarreling factions within Islam decide that they both have common enemies and common goals so they need to work together to accomplish their mutual objectives. It is the classic Arab proverb "The enemy of my enemy is my friend." The only factor missing in the Middle East equation is a strong charismatic leader who can galvanize and unite these different factions and it is only a matter of time before such a person emerges.

Chapter 15

What Drives Cultural Change

Certainly technology drives cultural change since it spreads culture at a much more rapid rate through electronic and social media. Cultural change can originate at the top levels of society or the bottom (the grassroots). Christianity was a grassroots movement that spread despite persecution by the Roman Empire until it was declared the official religion by Emperor Constantine in 312 A. D. If a grassroots movement is strong enough and has staying power, it will eventually win the support of the rulers. Christianity had to exist in the shadows for 280 years until Constantine established it as the State religion. The Protestant Reformation originated at the top when monarchs and rulers in Scandinavia, England and Germany adopted reformed doctrines. The common people resisted the Reformation but the rulers forced it down on them through a combination of laws, persecution and incremental changes. The American Civil Rights movement was a grassroots effort that succeeded when the Federal Government declared its support through legislation and the use of Federal troops (the integration of Little Rock High School in Little Rock, Arkansas in 1957 and the integration of the University of Mississippi in 1962). Had the Federal Government not intervened and left it up to the individual southern states, civil rights would still have evolved albeit slowly and over a period of decades. Some southern states in the 1960s proved that they could suppress demonstrators with a brutality not normally associated with the United States.

Cultural change in the United States is dependent upon four primary entities: universities, the media, the entertainment industry and the Federal Government. The first three are molders of public opinion and the government takes its cue from them. This is evident in the rapid acceptance of Gay Rights and same sex marriage. Just a few decades ago there were anti-sodomy laws on the books in every State. Terms like *queer* and *faggot* were freely used to describe homosexuals. The entertainment industry worked hard to conceal the homosexuality of popular entertainers like Rock Hudson and Liberace. Gays and Lesbians capitalized on the Civil Rights movement that first secured full equality for Blacks and then women. They also benefitted from the decline of religion and the rise of moral relativism in society. In the past, homosexuality was judged in accordance with the strong biblical and religious prohibitions against homosexual activity. As the cultural elites in the media, the universities, the entertainment industry and the government became increasingly hostile to traditional values, including Christianity, Gays and Lesbians enjoyed a rapid increase ins in cultural acceptance and approval.

In a democracy cultural changes begin with an appeal to fairness and civil rights. Politicians jump on these Civil Rights issues to get votes and if it is a popular social topic they will embrace it, legalize it and force it down on unwilling members of the society through legislation.

Social pressure through the weapon of Political Correctness plays a decisive role in driving cultural change. Critics of a popular cultural change face repercussions in the workplace and other public forums if they voice opposition to a popular social movement. Political Correctness silences some and brainwashes others into submission and acceptance.

There is one common denominator in play here: Cultural change will not come about without government support since government has legislative authority to enable, enforce or inhibit cultural change.

Can grassroots cultural changes occur in a non-democratic society? Yes, but only if the rulers go along with it as was the case with Christianity in the early 4ᵗʰ century Roman Empire. An example of this in recent history was the "Prague Spring" in 1968 when Czechoslovakian President Alexander Dubcek implemented a series of reforms that the grassroots wanted. As a Communist dictator he could have refused -- as most of dictators do -- and turned the army and police loose on those seeking reform. The Prague Spring did not last because the Soviet Union, which controlled Eastern Europe at the time, opposed the changes and sent in the Soviet Army to restore the Communist version of order. In 1990, Soviet Premier Mikhail Gorbachev responded to the strong dissident movement within the Soviet Union and ended Communism. If he had taken the hard line he could have used the Soviet military to maintain the Communist dictatorship. In both cases –

Dubcek and Gorbachev -- the leaders were motivated by a sense of right and morality. Gorbachev acted under political and economic pressure as well but he did possess a sense of justice not found in his predecessors. Instances like these, however, are extremely rare in dictatorships.

Certain social movements that gain traction in democracies -- abortion, physician assisted suicide, same sex marriage and legalized drugs -- are not healthy for a society and are symptoms of cultural decay. Abortion and physician assisted suicide are both forms of murder and cheapen and diminish the value of life in the culture. Physician assisted suicide runs the risk of a slippery slope that will eventually allow the immediate family or legal guardians -- even doctors -- to make that decision for an ailing family member. Same sex marriage is designed to end marriage as an institution and possibly open the door for polygamy, polyandry and incestuous marriages. (See chapter 5)

Legalized drugs destroy human lives. Marijuana is now legal in two states; eventually, it will be legal in all States. That opens the door for legalization of cocaine and heroin. Totalitarian regimes recognize the dangers of these social dysfunctions although China uses forced abortion as a means of population control, not a a "reproductive right." One society's tyranny is another's right.

Social changes in democracies always move Left. This will eventually make it impossible for any political party representing traditional values to win national office.

In democracies VOTES are the ultimate driver of social change. And how do you get votes? You pander to anything the electorate wants. Much of the social change in democracies is manufactured to gain as many votes as possible. We have to differentiate between basic (natural) human rights that should be protected and enforced such as equal treatment under the Law for all citizens -- and government generated rights -- abortion, same sex marriage, physician assisted suicide, legalized drugs, and "pathways to citizenship" for illegal immigrants -- are "rights" that have no intrinsic value beyond pandering for votes.

Conclusion

The best analogy of democracy is *The Time Machine,* a novel (1895) by H.G. Wells, a committed socialist. In the book, a time traveler travels forward to the year 802,701 and finds humanity divided into two species, The Eloi and the Morlocks. The Eloi do nothing but play all day and the Morlocks meet their needs for food, clothing and shelter. The Eloi are totally dependent on the Morlocks. But the Morlocks are not looking for votes-- they use the Eloi as their food supply. The Morlocks are literally doing to the Eloi what Secular Progressive (Democratic) politicians are figuratively doing to the culture -- devouring it into oblivion to satisfy their insatiable hunger for votes and power. Like the Eloi, we are only too willing to help them in return for Entitlements which often equate literally to food, clothing and shelter. We don't seem to mind just as the Eloi didn't seem to mind, and like the Eloi

We are committing cultural suicide.